Suvajra **The Wheel a**

The author was born Morgan Findlay in Scotland in 1952. He worked in medical laboratories for eight years before taking ordination into the Western Buddhist Order in 1978. For the next eleven years he taught Buddhism and meditation at the Manchester Buddhist Centre where he was chairman. He now lives and works at Padmaloka retreat centre in Norfolk. After teaching tours amongst the Buddhist community of western India, he twice visited Dhardo Rimpoche gathering material for this biography.

Suvajra **The Wheel and the Diamond**

The Life of Dhardo Tulku

Windhorse Publications

Published by Windhorse Publications
136 Renfield Street
Glasgow G2 3AU

©Windhorse Publications 1991

Cover design Dhammarati
Printed by Biddles Ltd
Guildford, Surrey

British Library Cataloguing in Publication data
Suvajra, Dharmachari, 1952—
The Wheel and the Diamond
1. Buddhism
I. Title
294.3923092

ISBN 0-904766-48-9

Contents

This book is dedicated to the memory of
Dhardo Rimpoche and all those whom he inspired to
follow the Bodhisattva Path

Preface

This book is a biography of the Tibetan monk, Thubten Lhundup Legsang, who was known as Dhardo, or Dhando, Rimpoche. He died on 24 March 1990 at the age of seventy-three. The publication of this book marks the anniversary of his death.

Dhardo, or Dhando, is a contraction of Dhartsendo, the town in eastern Tibet where he was born, while 'Rimpoche' is the Tibetan honorific, applied to lamas, meaning 'Greatly Precious One'. As a boy, Dhardo Rimpoche was recognized as the incarnation, or *tulku*, of a chief abbot of the famous Drepung Monastery in central Tibet. Thus he was also known as Dhardo Tulku. As such he was the thirteenth in his line.

He was raised and educated within the classical Tibetan monastic system, but in 1949 he left Tibet to become abbot of the Tibetan monastery at Bodh Gaya. Then, for forty years, he lived in Kalimpong, in northern India, where he founded an orphanage and school for Tibetan refugees and was the abbot of a local monastery. While there, he met and befriended an English-born Buddhist monk, Sangharakshita. The two men had been brought up in entirely different cultures; they differed in age and nationality, and they had been ordained into different strands of the Buddhist tradition. But their friendship was to influence many of the people, both Eastern and Western, who surrounded them.

Sangharakshita returned to the West, and in 1967 founded his own Buddhist movement: the Friends of the Western Buddhist Order. In 1978 I was ordained into the

Western Buddhist Order, and took the name Suvajra. I am a Dharmachari, a follower of the Buddha's path. My fascination with the 'traditional' Buddhist world and things Tibetan culminated in a pilgrimage, in the winter of 1985–6, to the sacred Buddhist places of India, and to Dhardo Rimpoche. The story of that journey is another book in itself, but it was then that I became involved in a chain of events which has led to the writing of this biography.

I had thought for some time that we should get some record of Dhardo Rimpoche speaking about his life, and I was delighted to find that another member of the Western Buddhist Order, Satyapala, had already begun work on such a venture. Before leaving for India, I offered to ask Rimpoche about any areas that Satyapala had not yet explored; Sangharakshita also gave me a list of twenty-five further questions to put to him.

In the course of the two days I spent with Rimpoche, I was able to learn a great deal. I followed this up with several letters and another visit in January 1988. Satyapala was by now unable to do much more work on the project. I nevertheless thought that someone should engage in some serious research in order to furnish a future biographer with the necessary information. I therefore started to hunt through my stock of books on Tibet, to comb systematically the library of the Western Buddhist Order, and to examine several large and aged collections of photographs of Tibet. This was a most absorbing period; I seemed to be living in traditional Tibet for stretches at a time, and I could speak of little else. Slowly, things came together and I began to write batches of letters to Tibet, China, and India for more information. Eventually, I had almost enough for a biography.

But by now I realized that *I* now knew more than anyone else about the subject of that biography. I also realized that if I did not make a start, Rimpoche might never see the finished work. I initially aimed to have a completed first draft to show Rimpoche when I visited him for a third time in March 1990. But as things turned out, because of other commitments, I had not even started writing by that date. I therefore travelled out armed with a final sheaf of questions.

The day before I flew to India, however, Rimpoche had a serious stroke. I knew that I could certainly not contribute any additional strain by interrogating him about his life, and instead decided to visit Nepal. I was still there when Dhardo Rimpoche died, four weeks after the stroke. I attended the funeral ceremonies in Kalimpong and made offerings on behalf of Sangharakshita and the Western Buddhist Order. Although I felt sadness, my overwhelming feeling was one of gratitude for the inspiration Dhardo Rimpoche had given me to practise the Buddha's teachings. I knew immediately that I would have to bring the biography to completion, as a tribute to him, and so that the example of his life might be an encouragement to others in their practice.

I hope the appeal of this book will be broader than that of some of the hagiographies which are often found in the Tibetan tradition. I have found it necessary to create the context for Dhardo Rimpoche's life within both Tibetan history and that branch of the Buddhist tradition now popularly called Tibetan Buddhism. Dhardo Rimpoche exemplifies what we have to learn from the Tibetan tradition—just as that tradition was the context within which the pattern of his life makes sense.

I have also found it necessary to start this biography with an account of the life of the previous Dhardo Tulku, in whose wake Rimpoche was raised. The previous *tulku* was a powerful personality, a very religious man who did not hesitate to use his considerable political influence. This should suggest that the spiritual life as conceived in the Buddhist tradition is not something practised solely within the confines of monastic cloisters. It is an engagement with, and a response to, the issues which life presents. Perhaps it will also suggest that sense of continuity which Rimpoche himself felt very strongly, and which served to inspire and enrich his life.

Many people helped me to research this biography. I would first like to thank those who interviewed Rimpoche: Dharmacharis Nagabodhi, Satyapala, Shantiprabha, Kulamitra, and Kuladeva. I also found indispensable the videotaped material provided by Dharmachari Mokshapriya and the translation work of Dharmachari Aniruddha, Tsering Dhondrup, and Ventul Rimpoche.

Background information for many parts of the book came from a number of sources: Geshe Jampel Thardo in Canada, Phuntsog Wangyal of the Tibet Foundation, and Geshe Thubten Jimpa and Gedun Tharchin of Ganden Monastery. I would also like to thank the Western Buddhist Order, at Padmaloka, and the Manjushri Institute, at Conishead, for the use of their libraries, and the Director of the Tibetan Library of Works and Archives. Gill Gebur of the India Office Library and Frank Treguier of Foundation Alexandra David-Neel, in Digne, France, helped by searching through their photographic archives, the latter giving permission to use the photograph of Dorje Drak Gompa. H.E. Richardson, the last British Government Resident in Lhasa, clarified a number of historical points. Dr Gyurme Dorje provided information regarding Dhartsendo and the two monasteries which are mentioned in Chapter Two, and translated the prayer for Rimpoche's rebirth. Dharmachari Alayavajra also helped in the preparation of the glossary.

In Kalimpong little would have been accomplished without the consistently willing help of Rimpoche's secretary, Jampel Kaldhen. His translation made all my interviews possible. He also did a lot of research in order to answer my many obscure questions, and cleared up my misconceptions. His family were also of great help when I interviewed them. Rimpoche's doctor Kushog Lhawangla and his friend Tashi Dorje, the dance-master, gave me much information about Rimpoche's last days.

In the great rush to complete the manuscript for publication on the anniversary of Rimpoche's death, many people put themselves at my disposal. I would first like to thank my own community at Padmaloka, Norfolk, who shut me in my caravan for a month and took over my usual duties, intercepting and dealing with telephone calls. As well as doing some typing, Ralph Worfolk and Clive Simpson helped clarify my English.

Dharmachari Subhuti pushed, prodded, and encouraged me to complete the text in time for what I considered to be an impossible deadline, and gave his time freely to help improve my English. The Venerable Sangharakshita, likewise, was a great encouragement in that he had faith that I could produce the text. He also read the manuscript in its earlier stages and suggested several improvements and corrections. But the real credit for finishing the text on time must go to Simon Blomfield who had the mammoth task of turning my often very poor and sloppy use of English into something more polished, he also restructured the text so as to improve its flow. Dharmacharis Nagabodhi and Shantavira also improved the text significantly, and pushed it through publication at breakneck speed.

Introduction: *Turning the Wheel*

Dhardo Rimpoche was cremated at his monastery in Ghoom, in the hills above Darjeeling. When the cremation *stupa* was opened, it was found that two of the many symbols which had been placed inside had survived the conflagration. These were the symbols which Dhardo Rimpoche had held most dear, and they now seemed to provide a mute testament on his life. There was a Dharmachakra wheel, representing the ceaseless activity of the teaching and practice of Buddhism, which was set in motion by the Buddha two-and-a-half millennia ago. And there was a *vajra*, a diamond-sceptre, suggesting the immutable purity of the Absolute, and the unshakeable strength of inner realization.

After these symbols had been exposed to view, Ventul Tulku climbed inside the *stupa* to recover the ashes and remaining bones from the metal framework which had held Rimpoche's corpse above the pyre. A Tibetan helper and I were below with an outstretched cloth to catch any escaping fragments of bone. A little later, back in Kalimpong, the remains were installed in a shrine above Rimpoche's school. They were wrapped in silken cloth, surmounted by a multi-coloured, five-pointed crown, and ceremonially installed on a specially constructed throne.

After everyone who had made offerings to the relics had left, I looked at the debris around me. Mud had been trailed in and was now ground into the floor, along with a quantity of spilled rice; tables were strewn with porcelain bowls of half eaten rice—the apricots they had contained had toppled onto the grime below. I set about

restoring the room to a semblance of order, sweeping the
debris out into the dark and rainy night. I cleaned the china
cups, with their oriental saucers and jewel-encrusted lids,
until they looked like miniature pagodas. I replenished the
butter lamps which had spluttered and died, and I lit fresh
bundles of incense. Finally, I sat in the golden radiance of
a hundred newly lit butter-lamps, while pine incense
smoke coiled in the warmth. Flickering shadows were cast
on the mountains of offering scarves which lay before the
gorgeous brocade of Dhardo Rimpoche's robes. I was left
alone with my memories of him and the lessons which his
life had taught.

In the previous few hours I had seen much of the exiled
Tibetan community of Kalimpong, as many of its members
had filed through in devout respect. I had witnessed one
of the most important rituals of that community: the
cremation and the interment of the ashes of one of its
principal teachers. And I had participated in rituals which
dated back a thousand years. I felt privileged to have been
present and to have been able to forge a personal connection with Dhardo Rimpoche, my teacher's teacher. But my
good fortune was only possible at the price of the tragedy
which had brought these people to Kalimpong.

For many people, Tibet still means mountains and yaks,
monasteries and monks. Whilst this picture contains large
elements of myth and fantasy, it is true that Tibetan culture
is unique and precious. Since the adoption of Buddhism,
in the ninth century CE,[1] culture and religion have inter-
woven to such an extent that it is hardly possible to separate one from the other. An astonishing one-seventh of the
population was involved, to one extent or other, with the

---

[1] Buddhists and other non-Christians do not use the abbreviations
AD—'Year of our Lord'—and BC. They refer to years under the accepted
dating convention as either CE (Common Era) or BCE (before Common
Era).

monastic system. Conversely, despite efforts to reform the country, the economy was still feudal and trade was, for the most part, conducted by barter. Technology had made virtually no impression, and education trained people for only two vocations: the ecclesiastical life and government service. Everyone else worked the land. In this century, however, Tibet has been rudely visited by some of the harshest aspects of the outside world. It has seen one British and two Chinese invasions. The most recent of these, in 1951, effectively ended her independence.

In 1959 a popular rebellion against the Chinese was countered by the systematic oppression of the Tibetan people, their culture, and their religion. The Dalai Lama fled, government officials and leading monks were arrested and shot or tortured. Monasteries were bombed, sacred images destroyed, and thousands of ordinary people lost their lives. Children were separated from their parents and sent off for 'education' in far parts of China, never to see their families again. Men and women were sent to work-camps all over China, while Chinese people were offered land in Tibet at good prices with subsidies and special tax considerations. During the Cultural Revolution of 1967, the remains of Tibetan Buddhism were ground to dust and those adherents not already forced underground were punished, tortured, or killed.

Many Tibetans chose to try their luck in exile, and refugees poured out of Tibet, across dangerous and little known passes, into Nepal, Sikkim, and Bhutan during the weeks following the military take-over; hundreds of thousands more have fled during the subsequent years. They brought with them shreds of religious scroll paintings, pages of sacred texts, and even huge Buddha images which had been sawn into manageable sizes for re-assembly in India. The Dalai Lama set up a government-in-exile in India, and his people were resettled in several

locations across the length and breadth of the sub-
continent. Many were accepted into neighbouring Nepal,
Sikkim, and Bhutan. They remain desperately poor, but
this has not been their greatest hardship. They are now
confronted by the threatened destruction of their culture
and, with it, the extinction of their unique form of
Buddhism.

In Tibet today, some practice of Buddhism is still permitted, but meditation and teaching (which are the very
heart of Buddhist practice) are banned. To be a monk or
nun is by no means easy, and many still flee Tibet with
tales of persecution and torture. Meanwhile, a generation
of Tibetans has grown up under the influence of
Communism; a generation, too, has grown up outside
Tibet in a very different world. Inside the country, the
Tibetans are being swamped by Chinese; outside, they are
only one people in an ocean of others. How much longer,
they wonder, can what is distinctively Tibetan survive?

It is clear to all that if Tibetan Buddhism is to be saved
from extinction it has to be done by the exiles. Thus,
although the Dalai Lama considers that his fight for the
freedom of his country is vitally important, the preservation of Tibet's unique form of Buddhism takes priority. He
has therefore encouraged the former abbots to re-establish
the principal monastic colleges. And he has encouraged
teachers to pass on the ancient lineages of rituals and
meditation practices. As the Tibetans see it, these lineages,
which only very few accomplished masters understand
thoroughly, are in danger of being lost for want of accomplished pupils. Then, too, there is the vast heritage of
artistic skills and crafts which developed around the
Tibetan Buddhist system, and which is indispensable to
Tibetan ritual.

Perhaps most important of all is the education of the
ordinary people. Without some knowledge of Tibetan

language, art, and history, they cannot hope to understand the great wealth of the Dharma as it has been preserved in Tibet. But here lies the dilemma: what do you chose to teach to children who are being brought up, not in a medieval, agrarian society, but in a modern, technological world? Which elements of a traditional religious culture can be preserved when religious and spiritual values seem to be not only out of step with the modern world but even in conflict with it? In such materially pressing times, it can seem to many that Western science and technology have more security to offer than do mantra and prayer.

Dhardo Rimpoche was concerned with these issues from the start, and he dedicated his life to addressing them. He had been educated in the traditional monastic system, but he found himself in India three years before the invasion of 1951. He could see clearly what was coming, long before most others, and was prepared in advance. The wheel of the Buddha's teaching had been revolving in Tibet for over a thousand years; his concern was to keep it turning.

1 The Indo-Tibetan Buddhist Cultural Institute

Much knowledge, and much skill in arts and crafts,
A well-learnt discipline, and pleasing speech—
This is the most auspicious sign of all.

To give in charity, live righteously,
To help one's kindred in the time of need,
and to do spotless deeds that bring no blame—
This is the most auspicious sign of all.[1]

At long last, on a bright, cold day in January 1986, I arrived at Dhardo Rimpoche's School in Kalimpong. It had been a long journey and I had been taken ill in Calcutta, but, eventually, I had made my way up the slither of India which worms its way between Sikkim, Bhutan, Nepal, Bangladesh, and Chinese Tibet. I had heard much about the Indo-Tibetan Buddhist Cultural Institute School and much about the old Tibetan who ran it, but, looking around, there did not seem to be very much to see. There was a small, two-storeyed stone building rather precariously balanced on the steep side of a deep water channel; the rest was a ramshackle collection of wooden huts. I later discovered that the stone building housed Dhardo Rimpoche's quarters and offices, while the school was accommodated in the huts. I was also disappointed to find that I had arrived during the school holidays and that only a few children were present.

I was greeted by a smiling, broad-faced Tibetan who introduced himself as Jampel Kaldhen, secretary to

[1] *Mangala Sutta*, trans. Sangharakshita

Dhardo Rimpoche and headmaster of the school. He took me to a little wooden bungalow where he lived with his family. After we had formally greeted one another I rather shame-facedly told him that I was sick with diarrhoea. He was immediately anxious to help. Mrs Kaldhen, he apologized, was away on pilgrimage at Bodh Gaya. She was receiving highly auspicious initiations from the Dalai Lama himself. But of course their youngest daughter, Zumkyid, and their eldest son, Jigmed, would look after me in her place. So while I lay down on their most comfortable chair, they fed me sweet tea and biscuits: 'Very, very nice! Indeed very good! Very kind for stomach!' Meanwhile several little children popped in and out of the lounge and peered with large, frank Tibetan eyes at the strange man from Britain. These were boarders, most of them orphans, whom the school had taken in, or children whose parents lived too far away for them to travel back for the holidays.

Soon after, I climbed the steps up the outside of the stone house for my first interview. I was a Buddhist from the Western Buddhist Order, and my own teacher, Sangharakshita, was himself British. Up to now, Kalimpong had been just an exotic name that cropped up in his recollections of his time in India; Dhardo Rimpoche had been a picture on a shrine and the alluring name of one of Sangharakshita's principal teachers. But my pilgrimage to the holy places of northern India and Nepal had, finally, brought me here. In the ante-room, ignoring Jampel's protests, I removed my shoes in accordance with the usual Buddhist custom, and prepared my offering scarf. I was then ushered into a small room whose floor was so bitterly cold that I immediately regretted not having listened to Jampel.

Dhardo Rimpoche was sitting on a box-like couch against the far wall underneath a tiny brocade canopy.

Behind him hung three scroll paintings, or *thangkas*. To his right was the smiling, thousand-armed figure of Avalokiteshvara, the embodiment of Compassion; to his left was the radiant and beautiful female figure of White Tara, embodiment of Wisdom and bestower of blessings; between them, directly behind Rimpoche, a painting depicted a host of figures seated on a tree of lotuses.

Dhardo Rimpoche was in his late sixties. He had a grey moustache, a wispy beard, and virtually no hair—all of which gave him a highly oriental appearance. His eyes were sharp and clear, and they narrowed in wrinkling creases as they were taken up into a cheery and enormously welcoming smile. My pilgrimage had arrived at its culmination.

Although it is more customary to perform kneeling prostrations, or the kowtow, I made three full-length prostrations before Rimpoche. Nothing less could have given expression to my feelings at that moment. As I rose I presented Rimpoche with the traditional white offering scarf. He beckoned me with his extended hand to sit down. Taking this for a more familiar sort of welcome, I grasped it in a handshake. The gasps of astonishment from Jampel, and the others who were present told me that I had made my first social gaffe, but Rimpoche himself, though surprised, did not seem in the least perturbed. He returned the handshake and continued to beckon me to a seat by the window.

At first, it was all I could do to contain my excitement. Every time I tried to speak I burst out laughing—and every time I did so Rimpoche joined in himself. Eventually I was able to tell him how long I had wanted to visit and that I was delighted to be there. He welcomed me and, having heard that I had been sick in Bodh Gaya and Calcutta, asked after my health. When he enquired after Sangharakshita's health I took the opportunity to present the gift with which Sangharakshita had entrusted me. It was an expensive pen with a modern filling mechanism about which Sangharakshita had taken the trouble to write a carefully-worded letter:

> Dear Suvajra, This afternoon I went into Norwich and was able to get a rather fine, gold-plated pen for Dhardo Rimpoche. It is of a new type, and you may have to show him how to fill it. Basically, after removing the cap one unscrews the pen and then fills it by screwing the plunger down towards the nib and then unscrewing it in the reverse direction. I hope this makes sense.

Rimpoche took great care in opening the package (carefully keeping the wrapping paper lest it come in handy) and gave a series of 'Ooh's of delight when he discovered what it contained. He took the long strip of complex instructions from the box and passed them, without a second look, to his secretary, who examined them earnestly. Letting out several more 'Ooh's, Rimpoche dismantled the pen and discovered how to operate the filling mechanism without the least help from myself or the string of instructions. This was clearly a capable man who, I was later told, often made little table lamps and thought nothing of installing electric cables. Now, fully satisfied that he knew how the pen worked, he admired it lovingly and clipped it inside the collar of his inner shirt alongside another one, his working pen. As a gift from Sangharakshita, the new pen was so precious that he would never use it. After his death it was found carefully packed in its velvet and silk-lined box.

Rimpoche seemed to have a disarming simplicity and unaffected directness. Already, within those first moments, I had seen some of his most characteristic qualities: his earnest concern about my health, his practicality, and his sense of the relativity of social conventions.

Only when it seemed appropriate did I take things further by asking him about the text he had been reading when I came in. He told me that it concerned *Shunyata*, or 'Emptiness', one of the most profound teachings in Buddhism. This seemed to take the conversation much further. His answer made me pause for a moment. I thought of my own difficulties in attempting to combine a busy life running the Manchester Buddhist Centre with meditation and other kinds of formal Buddhist practice. I therefore asked him how he reconciled the demands of the worldly activities involved in running a school and monastery with those of formal Buddhist practice. His answer was straightforward but, nonetheless, astonishing.

Dhardo Rimpoche's daily programme ran as follows. He regularly rose between 4.00 and 4.30a.m. He washed and dressed while visualizing himself in the form of a deep blue, bull-headed figure called Vajrabhairava (or 'Diamond-Terror'), the wrathful form of Manjushri, embodiment of Wisdom. At the same time he recited prayers of purification and repeated mantras. He continued to do this while cleaning his teeth which, consequently, took between forty and fifty minutes. He then ate a light breakfast and sat for a period of formal meditation.

This started with a systematic reflection on his purpose; only when he was fully satisfied that he was not seeking blessings or personal merit would he proceed to the full practice. As a prelude to this, he engaged in an examination of any unskilful actions he had committed, and made a ritual confession of them. In this purified state he recited the traditional Refuges and Precepts, committing himself to the ideals of Buddhism and to the practice of ethics. He then visualized Tsongkhapa, the fourteenth century founder of his monastic sect, with his two main disciples, and recited a prayer on the 'Three Principles of the Path'. Here, he symbolically established all beings in a state of purity by visualizing himself surrounded by an infinite host of beings and imagining them bathed in light which poured from his heart.

Next, in what he called the 'main meditation' of the morning, Rimpoche visualized two Bodhisattvas in female form: White Tara who is immaculate and radiant, seated in meditation posture, and Green Tara who has one foot stepping down into the world. Rimpoche concluded his period of meditation by reciting all the mantras for which he might be called upon to give initiation. He also found half an hour every morning to do some gardening among the rows of potted plants on his roof-top. If there was any time left over he would study until lunch. This was how he spent the first six hours of each day. Rimpoche regarded these hours of spiritual practice as the indispensable basis for the cultivation of the insight and compassion from which everything else in his life derived.

After this, his time belonged to the school, and, though he did not teach, he did whatever administrative work was required to ensure that everything was running smoothly. Over the years the school had often been desperately short of money, and much of his time had had to be spent trying to find savings, or working out how to make the tiny income stretch further. Only very recently, due to help from Western Buddhists, had these problems started to recede. Visitors knew that this was the time when Rimpoche was available to see them, and in recent years they had been coming in increasing numbers. Although he was gradually passing on responsibility to Jampel Kaldhen, this was often a busy time of the day. But, no matter how busy he was, he always had time for the children. He took photographs of each child who attended the school. For a long time he would also develop and print these pictures, making one copy for the child and one for himself. Latterly, however, the task had become so time-consuming that Jampel had insisted that he develop only the negatives and give them to others for printing. Each evening the head pupil came to tell Rimpoche that the boarders were gathered for the evening chanting session. He joined the children in a class-room and listened while they chanted a traditional text lasting nearly half-an-hour. If a new child was having difficulties, Rimpoche would sit by them and help them with the Tibetan script. The children told me that they loved this time when Rimpoche was with them.

After a light evening meal he performed the Tsongkhapa ritual again, then two more elaborate meditation practices. He concluded with a *puja* in which he made offerings on behalf of the dead. He usually finished between 11.00 and 11.30p.m, but, if school duties had been particularly time-consuming, he might not finish before 1.00a.m; nevertheless, Rimpoche considered it important to maintain his practice without missing a single day.

A young, runny-nosed girl brought in two large thermos flasks, from one of which she filled my mug with sweetened Indian tea while from the other she poured steaming-hot buttered tea into Rimpoche's rather splendid white porcelain red-rimmed mug. She ran out again, but some time later she and a few others could be heard whispering and laughing with each other in the vestibule until someone came and shoo'ed them away. This was a glimpse of what I had missed by arriving in the holidays. I had been told that the children at this school seemed remarkably happy; I had been told that they were deeply versed in the ancient traditions and that they were also able to understand the modern world. I had been warned that the school would be different in many ways to any other I might have seen and that it was also different in a few very important respects from any other school for Tibetan children in India.

The Chinese had marched into Lhasa in 1950. Already, some wealthy Tibetans had begun to leave Tibet or send their children and valuables to India for safety. Dhardo Rimpoche had realized that things would almost certainly get much worse: if the Chinese took over Tibet there would be a massive exodus of refugees to India. But he also saw that the real issue was to be the survival of Tibetan Buddhism and its culture. Children would grow up outside that culture; they would feel rootless. Worse than this, they would be without access to the Buddhism which was so deeply embedded in it and which their culture afforded. Rimpoche's earliest idea, therefore, was that his school should have half its time set aside for traditional subjects and half for subjects essential for growing up in the world in which the children now found themselves. Mornings were therefore set aside for Hindi, English, arithmetic, and so on, but afternoons were devoted to Tibetan writing, grammar and composition, Tibetan history, painting, dancing, and to the study of traditional stories outlining the importance of morality.

But in order for a school to be eligible to receive government grants and take part in national exams it was required that it follow a centrally prescribed curriculum. This would have entailed the loss of virtually all the traditional subjects, and Tibetan language would have been relegated to much shorter classes held only twice a week. The results of this policy can be seen today in the young Tibetans who are growing up with only a rudimentary grasp of their language, often unable to read it at all. Although this would not have been a problem in old Tibet (where many people had been illiterate) the future of Tibetan culture now depended on the refugees. For this reason, and despite great pressure to accept government backing, Dhardo Rimpoche held fast to his initial vision. Although, at times, the school was almost bankrupt, he managed, somehow, to keep it running until a secure financial basis could be found. The school was small and many of the pupils came from very humble backgrounds, but it embodied his vision for the future of the Tibetan people.

In 1959, after an unsuccessful revolt, Tibet had been taken fully under Chinese control and what has sometimes been called 'the Tibetan genocide'[1] began. Refugees poured in their thousands over the narrow Himalayan passes and into the towns of the foothills. Kalimpong, and its neighbouring town of Darjeeling, are at the southern end of one of the major routes out of Tibet. These towns were deluged by refugees. Cast out and homeless, shocked by the atrocities they had seen, they wandered through the streets begging for food, or sat by the roadside and sold their smallest possessions. Monks were redundant as well as homeless—and usually without a trade; if they were lucky they found labouring jobs breaking stones which would be used in repairing roads. Most unfortunate of all were the thousands of orphaned children.

Rimpoche's school had been able to respond to the needs of some of these people, and he had opened an orphanage to house some of the destitute children. The pattern of Rimpoche's life was thus established as a balance of social work, administration, and spiritual practice. This was a remarkable combination, and I hoped that in talking to Dhardo Rimpoche I would start to understand how his meditation and his practice of Buddhism had given rise to the school. I wanted to know why it was that he worked in such humble circumstances, in spite of his birth as a high ranking 'incarnate' lama.

[1] Tibetan genocide may seem a strong description, but this is how the International Commission of Jurists, reporting in 1959, described the activities of the Chinese Communists between 1951 and 1959.

As we sat drinking endless cups of tea I tucked my feet under me, out of the cold, taking care not to point them disrespectfully at Rimpoche. He sat in the same posture, so it was not until he rose that I noticed the pronounced stoop he had developed, probably as a result of years spent craning over the table before him. This table was covered by a dreadfully gaudy, pink plastic cloth with a red and orange design. On it was a brocade-covered box with a large pile of loose-leaf Tibetan texts which were adjuncts to his daily meditation and ritual. There was also a bell which might have been more at home in a hotel lobby, and an assortment of pens and pencils standing upright in a holder. There was a small fat bottle with a red screw-top containing something which looked like brown sand. A few white offering scarves were carefully draped over one corner of the table and there was something large, wrapped in cloth and looking for all the world like a dumpling. Scattered here and there were a few pieces of paper and an envelope.

Rimpoche seemed not to notice the cold which grew as the sun sank behind the steep hill. Already it was late afternoon, and in the relatively short time I had been there I had found out much. But there were other questions. There was the list of twenty-five questions that Sangharakshita had given me, and there were questions which I wanted to ask in order to understand Rimpoche more fully. I felt, in particular, that one could not really understand the significance of much of his early life without knowing about the previous Dhardo Rimpoche of whom he was a *tulku*, or 'incarnation'. I knew that Rimpoche's predecessor had been an outstanding figure, and I wondered how closely the two resembled each other. As the afternoon waned and the light darkened to a deep orange, Rimpoche talked. In imagination, at least for a short while, I left Kalimpong and, through Rimpoche's eyes, found myself in the Tibet of the last century.

2 The Greatly Precious Guru of Dhartsendo

*Be not afraid of good works, brethren. It is another name
for happiness, for what is desired, beloved, dear and
delightful—this word 'good works.'* [1]

Dhartsendo is situated just inside Tibet's eastern border
with China, in the Gyalrong district of Kham province. At
one time the Chinese called it Tachienlu, but now it has
been renamed Kangting and barely rates a mention in the
guidebooks. Once, though, it was the most important
trading town on the old Tea Road from China to Tibet, and
caravans of yaks and camels would ply back and forth
carrying silks, yak wool, musk, gold, silver, and the all-
important 'brick-tea'. At the end of the last century the
missionary Dr Susie Rijnhart limped back to Dhartsendo,
the sole survivor of a small, ill-fated expedition which had
attempted to reach Lhasa. During the Second World War
the French explorer Alexandra David-Neel was stranded
there for seven years. And pilgrims from Kham Province
traditionally left from Dhartsendo on the long trek to the
golden-roofed temples of Lhasa.

It was a small town whose narrow streets were normally
crowded with Tibetan and Chinese traders and with
monks from the surrounding monasteries. Some of these
monks came from Dorje Drak Gompa, the 'Giant Rock
Monastery' of Dhartsendo. This was not a large monastery
by Tibetan standards, but its history spanned several centuries. It had half-a-dozen buildings with pagoda-style,
red-tiled roofs, and nestled against a green scrub hillside.

[1] The Buddha—from *The Itivuttaka*, trans. F.L. Woodward, Oxford
University Press, 1948

Before its gatehouse ran a small river. Around the monastery walls were a number of large white *chortens*, or reliquary monuments, topped by red spires which were emblazoned with the crescent moon and the sun. On leaving Dhartsendo, a caravan of traders or pilgrims travelling to Lhasa would cross an old arched bridge and see Dorje Drak as Mary Taring in *Daughter of Tibet* described it, 'a picturesque lamasery with red buildings surrounded by tall trees'.

The monastery belonged to the Nyingmapas, who represented the oldest tradition of Tibetan Buddhism and drew their inspiration from Padmasambhava, the great Indian sage who had established Buddhism in Tibet in the eighth century by magically overcoming its demons. The Nyingmapas were second in numbers only to the Gelugpas, whose lineage derived from Tsongkhapa, the great reforming figure of the fourteenth century. Although there were other reformed schools, the Nyingmapas followed the old Tibetan translations of the Buddhist texts—hence the name Nyingmapa, meaning 'the Ancient Ones'.

It was popularly believed that when an important lama or spiritual teacher died he was able to *direct* his rebirth; he would then be 'rediscovered' as a young child and trained to take over his affairs from where he had left off. Teachings which he had entrusted to his disciples would be returned to him in his new life so that he could pass them on to the succeeding generation. Such lamas were called *tulkus,* and every monastery was headed by at least one. Indeed, some of the larger monasteries boasted many *tulkus,* some of whose emanations spanned many lifetimes. The lineage of Nyingmapa *tulkus* which had governed Dorje Drak derived from a great teacher—who had lived centuries previously—called Asanga Rajaputra. An account of his life is to be found in the Nyingmapa annals along with those of the five subsequent *tulkus.* Until recently their statues stood in the main meditation hall of Dorje Drak. Six more *tulkus* followed, of whom almost nothing is known, but the twelfth, who was probably born in 1834 or 1835, was a towering personality and a central figure in some of the most difficult times Tibet has seen. By the time he was forty, three Dalai Lamas had died before coming to power, and the country was ruled by a series of regents until he was sixty. But he became a trusted friend of the 'Great Thirteenth' Dalai Lama, and worked closely with him as Tibet struggled to survive two major invasions.

He was born the son of the Chief Minister of Chakla, and was quickly recognized as the *tulku* of Dorje Drak Gompa. Little is known about his childhood or education, but as a youth he was famed for his exceptional learning, and he took early control of the monastery. His fame reached the ears of the renowned Gelugpa lama, Lobsang Khyenrab Wangchen, who also came from Dhartsendo. When the young *tulku* was visiting central Tibet on pilgrimage, on his way to commence studies at his mother monastery, Khyenrab Wangchen invited him to visit him in Drepung Monastery.

His pilgrimage probably took place in 1856, just before the death of the eleventh Dalai Lama and during the regency of Reting Rimpoche. In Lhasa, he paid his respects at the main temple and travelled to Drepung Monastery some miles outside the city, where he was to receive his audience with Lobsang Khyenrab Wangchen. Drepung was the largest monastery in Tibet, almost a city in itself, nestling in the arms of a mountain. It was famed for its beauty, and contained hundreds of white buildings, many of which had gilded roofs and housed numerous meditation halls embellished with rich decorations. The main assembly hall could hold seven thousand of the monastery's monks, and its forest of brocade-covered pillars supported a roof as richly decorated as that of the Sistine Chapel. Discipline was strict, the standard of teaching was high, and it was maintained in healthy, but intense, competition with the smaller rival monasteries of Sera and Ganden. Over a hundred incarnate lamas ranked among its eight thousand monks, and a young *tulku*, no matter how important, from a small provincial Nyingmapa monastery, could hardly fail to be impressed.

The meeting with Lobsang Khyenrab Wangchen marked the turning point in his life, for he decided to stay at Drepung and study with the Gelugpas. Within a few years he had mastered the studies and debating techniques, and had passed the *geshe* exam with second to top place for the year. This change, from Nyingmapa to Gelugpa, was not entirely unprecedented. It was not uncommon for the Gelugpas to encourage the most promising lamas in other traditions to study in their monasteries in central Tibet in the hope that they might later have a reforming effect. Khyenrab Wangchen had himself been a prominent figure in this movement and the young *tulku* may also have been influenced by the non-sectarian approach which was gaining popularity in eastern Tibet. But his decision, nonetheless, represented a significant departure from tradition. Although the four main schools of Tibetan Buddhism overlap to a great extent in both practice and doctrine, they remain very different. In his eleven previous lives he had worked as the spiritual guide of a Nyingmapa monastery and of the people of Dhartsendo, but he was now increasingly to identify himself as a Gelugpa lama, and was never to return to Dorje Drak. He also received a new name; at Drepung he was known as Dhardo or Dhando Tulku—the *tulku* from Dhartsendo.

In due course, Khyenrab Wangchen became Ganden Tripa, head of the Gelugpa order; eventually he became regent. One of his first appointments was to make Dhardo

Tulku abbot of Loseling College. Loseling was the largest of the four colleges in Drepung, so this represented a considerable appointment for a lama who had only recently 'converted' from the Nyingmapas. Dhardo Tulku became well known both as a scholar and as an organizer. In time, he was the natural choice for the post of Khenpo Tripa, the senior abbot of Drepung Monastery, which was held for several years. Along with the chief abbots from Sera, Ganden, Reting, and three other, smaller monasteries near Lhasa, he had a large say in many governmental matters. Later, as the seniormost of the retired chief abbots, he worked for the Tsong-du, Tibet's National Assembly, where, it was said, no important matter could be decided in his absence.

In 1875 the twelfth Dalai Lama died before coming to power. The thirteenth was recognized shortly afterwards and, in the course of his childhood, he and Dhardo Tulku became very close. The last Dalai Lama to have ruled the country had died in 1806, but the thirteenth gained his majority in 1895 and, for the next nine years, engaged in a course of internal reform. He was only twenty, and highly idealistic. For a long time power had lain in the hands of old men; it was inevitable that the reforms would meet with resistance from the conservatives. Dhardo Tulku, his friend Lobsang Gyantsen (another Ganden Tripa), and his half brother, the Finance Minister, were well known as the main supporters of the Dalai Lama's reforms, and thus found themselves caught up in a factional conflict which concerned the future of Tibet.

The reforms were necessary if Tibet was to be able to confront the outside world from a position of strength, but the question of Tibet's external relations soon superseded everything else. Tibet had maintained its independence throughout the nineteenth century with the assistance of its geographical isolation and a centuries-old 'priest/protector' relationship with China, in which Tibet offered spiritual direction to the Chinese emperors in return for political protection. But China was itself struggling to confront the new powers of the modern world; in its weakened state it had failed to oppose a recent invasion of Tibet by Mongol tribes and, indeed, it was starting to reinterpret the old relationship as a peculiar form of vassaldom which afforded it proprietorial rights over Tibet. The Chinese were no longer friends.

This left Tibet confronting two vast and expanding European empires to the north and south; she was caught in between, subject to the suspicions of each and the ambition of both. To the north lay imperial Russia, about which the Dalai Lama knew almost nothing—although some links existed via the Buddhists of the Russian province of Buryat. To the south lay India, long since consumed by the British Empire which seemed to devour everything in its path. Upper Burma, itself a Buddhist country, had been forcibly annexed to the Empire only fifteen years previously. The British were concerned that were Tibet to make a hostile alliance, China or Russia might be brought within striking distance of India. Rumours developed around a Buryat lama, Dorjief, one of the Dalai Lama's tutors, whom they suspected of being a Russian spy. Fearing a Tibetan alliance with the Russians, and suspecting that there were armaments and perhaps even a Russian force in Lhasa, in 1904, during a border dispute, the British decided to send an armed force into Tibet under the command of Colonel Francis Younghusband.

Younghusband's force reached Lhasa leaving 2,700 Tibetan dead in its wake. The Dalai Lama had fled for Mongolia leaving regent Lobsang Gyantsen, Dhardo Tulku, and members of the National Assembly to negotiate a treaty. Little was known about Tibet's valuable natural resources; it was vast, remote, inaccessible, and undefendable. Britain had no serious imperial ambitions towards it, and was concerned only to pre-empt Russia and China. At gunpoint, Younghusband forced the Tibetan government to sign a treaty which agreed to pay reparations, conceded trading rights, admitted a British Resident, and gave Britain complete control over Tibet's foreign policy.

The Dalai Lama's exile was prolonged by a visit to Peking to discuss irregularities along the Chinese border, but when he arrived in Lhasa in 1909 he was only just ahead of a Chinese invasion force. Within weeks he had fled once more, this time to British territory, leaving government in the hands of the senior abbots. Dhardo Tulku was prominent among them as the seniormost retired abbot of Drepung and in possession of great authority within the monastery. But, before leaving, the Dalai Lama had called the abbots together and instructed them to take great care to ensure that there would be no hindrance to the study of the Dharma. As he departed, the Chinese invasion force came through Dhartsendo and down the old Tea Road, sweeping away all resistance.

It fell mainly to the governing abbots to devise a defence. The majority wanted the Tibetan army to be expanded by recruiting monks from Ganden, Sera, and Drepung who would be sent to meet the Chinese. Sera and Ganden complied, but much depended upon Dhardo Tulku. The decision was one of the most difficult he ever had to make; non-violence, the fundamental principle of Buddhist ethics, seemed to be at odds with the safety of the country. He pondered the issues carefully and took into consideration the Dalai Lama's parting advice. Finally Dhardo Tulku consulted the Gadong Oracle which, in trance, supported what now seemed the only decision which accorded with his principles. He would send money, but he would not send monks. This decision was greatly resented outside Drepung, and the old factional rivalries revived. Like Dhardo Tulku, many of the monks in Drepung came from eastern Tibet, close to the Chinese border, and it was suggested that they were reluctant to fight because of mixed loyalties, or because they feared Chinese retaliation against their families. Some felt that Dhardo Tulku had failed the country.[1]

Defences were swept aside and the Chinese Imperial Army marched into Lhasa. Dhardo Tulku and the new regent, Tsomo Ling Rimpoche, conducted negotiations, but these were quite different from those which they had held with the British. The Chinese considered Tibet a province of China, and the Tibetans their subjects; they wanted a permanent occupation and were prepared to enforce their claims ruthlessly. Dhardo Tulku knew that the maintenance of Tibetan independence was crucial to the survival of the Dharma. Its culture would otherwise become subservient to Chinese culture and, perhaps, be supplanted by it. His aim in the negotiations was therefore to stall rather than bargain, while the National Assembly pursued a policy of non-cooperation and obstruction. Ironically, Tibetans now found themselves hoping that the British would return to drive out the Chinese. But even these hopes were disappointed by a British concern not to prejudice its trade negotiations with China. Finally, as Tibet seemed to be veering perilously close to disaster, the hated Manchu Dynasty was overthrown by Republicans, and the Chinese troops in Lhasa deserted or took to looting. In the resulting confusion the Tibetans regained control, and the remaining Chinese were deported. By the end

---

[1] The present Dhardo Rimpoche was keen to point out that these accusations against Drepung, and especially the Loseling monks, were unjust. As a young man he had read the letters which the previous *tulku* wrote to the thirteenth Dalai Lama explaining the ethical basis of his decision.

of 1912 the Chinese forces in the eastern part of the country had been beaten back along the Tea Road, through Dhartsendo, and into China. The Dalai Lama returned to a tumultuous welcome. Those who had distinguished themselves during the invasion were rewarded—Dhardo Tulku was presented with a wealthy estate, called Tonga Shega, while a wealthy disciple gave him a small house in Lhasa which he used to entertain guests. In 1916 or 1917, with the government safely back in the hands of the Dalai Lama, Dhardo Tulku died at the age of eighty-two. As one of the most popular and influential figures in Tibet, his funeral was lavish. His funerary stupa was embellished with silver and gold and placed in Drepung monastery, where thousands of monks gathered before it to pay their final respects. A liturgy of praise and of petition for the speedy return of their beloved lama was chanted in base tones to the accompaniment of thunderous blasts from twelve-foot trumpets, the clash of cymbals, and the combined ringing of a thousand diamond-sceptred bells.

3   The Search For A Tulku

To be born a human being
Is rarer than a star that shines by day.
If blessed enough to win a human body,
Many will waste it by running after pleasures,
But few can tread the Path of Dharma.
Though hundreds the gate may enter,
Few can keep the disciplines.[1]

When a *tulku* dies, his disciples embark on a search for the young child as whom he has been reborn. After his crema-tion the remains are examined for portents and, in the case of an important *tulku*, the Dalai Lama and the State Oracles are consulted. When Dhardo Tulku's disciples consulted the Gadong Oracle-Priest he threw his scarf in the eastern direction. They asked, 'How far?' and the Oracle said, 'Very far!' The Dalai Lama was rather more helpful and advised the envoys to start in Dhartsendo which lay to the east, and with which Dhardo Tulku had had a connection over twelve life-times.

Bhagdo Dharshab, nephew of the previous *tulku* and steward of his estate, led a group of monks on the long journey to Dhartsendo. One day, they discovered a boy whom they recognized as Dhardo Tulku, but, just as they were preparing to take him to Lhasa, he died. However, it is said that a *tulku* may be reborn in three separate bodies, one representing the energies associated with his body, one representing his speech, and another representing his mind. This meant that although the first boy might have

[1] *The Hundred Thousand Songs of Milarepa*, trans Garma C.C. Chang, Shambala, 1977

been a genuine incarnation, there might also be others. Indeed, Bhagdo Dharshab was soon to discover a three-year-old boy who had told his mother that he had many monasteries far away, and that he had to go to them. When the monks approached, he called out 'here come my servants'. The monks asked questions on the Dharma and his answers were clear and accurate. They placed a number of objects before the child, and from among the bells, rosaries, drums, and cups he unerringly picked out the things that had belonged to the previous *tulku*. Finally, the monks found a few marks on the boy's body which they considered auspicious, and were convinced. Bhagdo Dharshab declared that the new Dhardo Tulku had been found.

In relating all this to me, Rimpoche obviously did not think it very important. He said that he was quite sure that the boy who had died was the mind incarnation of the previous *tulku* and that he was 'maybe' one of the others. He said that when he was very young he had had memories of his previous life, but they had faded away, like dreams. He had not *felt* like a great lama, although everybody had treated him as one. It nevertheless occurred to him that, despite his feelings, he should try to *act* like a *tulku* by developing wisdom and compassion. Over the course of time, he had *become* a Rimpoche. The title 'Rimpoche', meaning 'Greatly Precious One', is usually reserved for *tulkus*, but it may be applied to anyone who has progressed on the Buddha's Path. 'You too can become Rimpoches,' he told his visitors. All they had to do was to start acting with wisdom and compassion.

Wangdag, the boy's father, was part Tibetan and part Chinese, a prosperous merchant dealing in musk, medicine, gold, and silver, but most of all in silk. He was an expert in recognizing and buying high quality silks, and many of the highest lamas, from even quite far away, would order religious robes and garments only from him. He was a kind-hearted man, but he despised deception and, recently, when his business was prospering, he had grown very hot-tempered. Rimpoche's mother, Namyäs, came from a noble family presided over by his grandmother, Che-Den Namyäs. She had borne a son who had died young and a daughter who had become a nun, therefore Dhardo Rimpoche remained as their only son and sole heir. Although his identification as a *tulku* promised to bring the family fame and prosperity, Rimpoche's parents insisted that the monks must be mistaken. Letters were sent to the Dalai Lama—who confirmed that the boy was the new Dhardo Tulku and told the couple that they were in danger of hindering his spiritual potential and heaping up demerit for themselves. Reluctantly, Rimpoche's parents agreed to give the boy up on condition that he should stay in Dhartsendo for a few more years. It was therefore agreed that he would study at Nam Chöd Gompa, the local Gelugpa monastery, and that he would commence his main studies in central Tibet when he was nine, at which time he would be formally enthroned.

At Nam Chöd his first teacher, or 'Root Guru', was Jampa Rimpoche, the son of a local chieftain, who had studied at Drepung and become a disciple of the previous Dhardo Tulku. Even at the age of four, Rimpoche had to rise at 4.00a.m. to memorize eight or ten lines of verse. Then he had to recite everything he had learned and could not have his morning tea or breakfast until he had completed the entire recitation. After breakfast came reading and writing until noon, and then he could play until 4.00p.m. That was followed by more recitation and chanting; he had to learn the various rituals which a *tulku* was required to perform. According to his mother he was a very sensitive and kind boy, but Rimpoche also remembers that, although always quick to learn, he was, in some ways, just like the other boys. He was often naughty and came in for quite a few beatings.

Dhardo Rimpoche's first taste of meditation came with his initiation into a visualization of the wrathful, bull-headed figure of Vajrabhairava, 'the Diamond-Terror'. Vajrabhairava is the wrathful form of Manjushri, the Bodhisattva of Wisdom, and the practice associated with him is one of the very highest of the Anuttara Yoga of the esoteric Tantra. He is an awe-inspiring, hybrid figure with nine faces, sixteen legs, and thirty-four arms. He is greatly revered within the Gelugpa school, and practices associated with him were encouraged by Tsongkhapa, its founder. This meditation is said to remove all hindrances to the spiritual path and to engender wisdom. Vajrabhairava is dark blue, and the principal head which stares back at those who gaze upon him is that of a bull. He is also known as Yamantaka, the slayer of Death. The meditation made such an impact on Rimpoche that he continued to practise it until the end of his life. Jampa Rimpoche also took him to meet eminent lamas from other sects who lived in the area, in particular leading members of the Shakyapa sect from whom he received *trui* or blessing-water and long-life initiations. Remembering their kindness and his own connection with the Nyingmapas, Dhardo Rimpoche grew up with great respect for genuine practitioners of the Dharma regardless of the tradition within which they practised.

In 1927 Rimpoche's family prepared to move to Lhasa. It was generally believed that with the birth of a *tulku* a family's 'worldly' activities began to fail, to be replaced by an increasing interest in the spiritual life. Wangdag's business had not been going well since Rimpoche's birth, but he was no longer bad tempered and had even stopped smoking. But as he became poorer and lived a simpler life, he became much kinder and started making offerings to

monks. Finally, upon moving to Lhasa, he gave up his
business and devoted himself more fully to a religious life.

Rimpoche remembered little of the journey through the
vast and dangerous wildernesses of eastern Tibet, or of the
staggering passes that their caravan had to traverse. But
his entry to Lhasa was unforgettable. He was greeted by
disciples of the previous *tulku*, and from within a few miles
of Lhasa thousands of monks from Drepung, Sera,
Ganden, and other monasteries lined the roads holding
offering scarves and lighted incense sticks. Almost the
whole city turned out to welcome him. Underneath the
Royal Umbrella reserved for high lamas Rimpoche found
himself with a complete entourage and, preceded by shrill
notes of monastic trumpets, entered the city. He made the
traditional visit to the ancient Jokang Temple, and, as had
his predecessor over seventy years previously, circum-
ambulated the city, received the blessings of the Dalai
Lama, and then made his first visit to Drepung.

The monastery was decorated with hundreds of brilliant banners of welcome, fluttering in the trees. His enthronement took place in the Great Assembly Hall, before
eight thousand monks including novices, treasurers,
geshes, abbots, *tulkus*, and the head of the Gelugpa Order.
As a token of respect he had to present gifts to all the
dignitaries and make a small donation to every monk (the
prospect of which had swollen the numbers beyond the
official limit). He had yet to discover the cost of these gifts,
the lavish food, and the endless rounds of buttered tea
which were costing his estate a small fortune.

But, with his enthronement, an even more powerful
influence was brought to bear. He was now officially
recognized as the thirteenth Dhardo Tulku and was living
among people who had vivid memories of his predecessor, including many who had been direct disciples. Most
of us are moulded to some extent by the influences of our

parents and teachers. They have expectations and hopes which we find hard to escape. We are influenced by their personalities, their achievements and failures, by their merits and demerits, their home-spun wisdom and their ignorance. Dhardo Rimpoche was faced with the formidable precedent set by his previous incarnation, and the expectations upon him were tremendous. He was often told: 'The previous *tulku* did this', 'The old Rimpoche did it that way.' Such expectations weighed heavily upon him, and he found that he was to be brought up more strictly than almost anyone else in the monastery.

But he was also to be the recipient of overwhelming devotion. People would come from far and near just to receive his blessing, to bow at his feet, and give him expensive offerings. Thus he was brought up in the twin environments of great strictness and overwhelming devotion. The former can warp the character and leave a legacy of rebelliousness, brooding resentment, and guilt; the latter can breed arrogance or irresponsibility. But the devotion to which Dhardo Rimpoche was exposed was directed to his position as an exemplar of the religious ideals of the Tibetans; the strictness took the form of an ethical training which was intended to provide the basis upon which he could engage in study and meditation and, eventually, live up to these expectations. However one may wish to explain the psychological processes which were invoked, the result was an outstanding individual who was both strong and outspoken, and keenly aware of his responsibilities to other people.

4 The Golden Roofed Monastery

*May I be continually cared for by a holy Spiritual Master
whose mind-stream abounds with good qualities of
scriptural knowledge and insight, whose senses are
calmed, who has self control, a heart of loving compassion
and the courage of mind to accomplish undauntedly the
purposes of others.*[1]

Drepung was the largest monastery in the world and had
all the bustling life of a small town. Most monks were
engaged in study or teaching, but others had to work; they
were cooks, tradesmen, builders, and servants of the more
prosperous monks. Some spent their time preparing giant
cauldrons of tea, others renewing butter-lamps. In the
daytime visitors, messengers, pilgrims, and traders
thronged the steep cobbled streets, but they returned to
Lhasa at nightfall leaving the monastery to the monks.
This was the world that Dhardo Rimpoche was joining
and in which he was to live for seventeen years. Drepung
was divided into four *tratsangs*, or colleges, called
Loseling, Deyang, Gomang, and Ngagpa; each of these
comprised many *khangtsens*, or 'house-divisions', which
monks joined according to the part of the country from
which they came. Loseling had twenty-three *khangtsens*,
the largest of which were Tsangpa, Phukang, and Tsara,
collectively known as 'The Three Ornaments of the Ear
and Nose'. Dhardo Rimpoche entered Tsangpa House.
    The Dalai Lama asked for names to be submitted for the

---

[1] Tsongkhapa, *The Prayer of the Virtuous Beginning, Middle and End*, from
Thurman, R., ed., *Life and Teachings of Tsongkhapa*, Library of Tibetan
Works and Archives, Dharamsala, India, 1982

post of tutor to the young *tulku*. Two of the men proposed were famous old *geshes* but, unusually, the Dalai Lama chose a monk called Yeshe Lhundup, who was in his early twenties and had yet to qualify. The older monks were at the height of their careers and might have died or become decrepit before Dhardo Tulku had completed his *geshe* studies. In contrast, by entrusting the younger man with the education of so important a *tulku*, Yeshe Lhundup was being challenged to excel in both study and teaching. A further consideration may have been that, as well as the required metaphysics and philosophy, he was familiar with Tibetan literature, prosody, composition, calligraphy, astrology, and history. The Dalai Lama was aware of the threat to Tibet's cultural traditions which the invasions of 1904 and 1911 had posed, and he placed great importance on safeguarding their future. In later years, Dhardo Rimpoche was very grateful for the breadth of the education he received from Yeshe Lhundup. As he told me, it had now fallen to him to preserve that tradition.

Yeshe Lhundup was born, just after the turn of the century, near Pempo, north of Lhasa, a famous centre of the old Kadam tradition. Some people considered Lhundup to be an incarnation of a sage called Geshe Sharawa, a disciple of Atisha, who was associated with the town. In two surviving photographs, taken when he was in his late thirties or early forties, he appears full of life and energy. His head is shaved, he has a full moustache, and his eyes shine out. One of Dhardo Rimpoche's former pupils, Geshe Jampel Thardo (who now lives in Canada) remembers him clearly:

'He was a very special, very peaceful lama. He was loved by young and old, by his students and by those who were not his students. Some people said that if they were nervous or sad they could visit him and feel peaceful immediately. It was not unusual, when a lama became famous, for some students of other colleges to become jealous. Then you would hear gossip and criticism, but it was different with Yeshe Lhundup. Nobody criticized him. He was like everybody's mother.'

A strong relationship began to grow between Dhardo Rimpoche and his guru, in whom he saw nothing but kindness, knowledge, and wisdom. When Yeshe Lhundup took his *geshe* exams a few years after commencing Rimpoche's tuition, his calibre was confirmed when he was ranked joint highest in the year (although, as a foreigner, the Mongolian lama with whom he had tied was granted precedence in the rankings). Dhardo Rimpoche's devotion seems to have grown steadily over the years and, not long before Rimpoche himself took the *geshe* examination, Jampel Thardo noticed it when he arrived at Drepung:

'Dhardo Rimpoche's guru-devotion was very special. Even if he did something very small, he would ask Geshe Yeshe Lhundup for permission. Sometimes people get angry or impatient with their teachers, and with so many people around this cannot be hidden. Yet people who saw him every day said that Rimpoche's face never changed. It always showed the signs of deepest respect. He was like a good son.'

Geshe Lhundup was equally devoted to his young pupil and was lax in neither love nor discipline. He was capable of explaining the loftiest teachings of Buddhism but he also had a down-to-earth and candid approach to ethics, which he regarded as an essential prerequisite for the study of the Buddhist texts. If one acted unethically it showed an insensitive mind polluted by greed, hatred, and delusion which as soon affected one's study as it did the people around. Rimpoche related that:

'My guru was very strict and used to scold us a lot. He used to beat me really severely, but as a result of this I studied well. I didn't feel angry that he beat me but I used to feel sad, thinking, "Why do I have to suffer so much?" When he beat me he would do it with a smile on his face and, at the same time, chant a traditional verse about skilful and unskilful action. Then he would explain to me what I had done wrong, why it was unskilful, and give me strong encouragement to get rid of the fault.'

Dhardo Rimpoche considered that it was good to be strict with young children, and especially with monks. In the case of a *tulku*, discipline had to be stricter still; although he may be reputed to have been a great lama, 'He is born of the womb so there will still be some delusion, unless and until he is properly trained'. Rimpoche contrasted traditional methods with contemporary ones:

'*Traditional* means that something has certain rules: suppose you are senior to me and you advise me to do something, I will definitely carry it out. And if I order my juniors to do something, they will automatically carry that out without questioning it. But in the modern way, when one asks someone to do something, they hesitate and first think "But what is *my* viewpoint?"'

Lhundup advised Dhardo Rimpoche not to think of himself as an important person because he was a recognized *tulku*, or to expect anything from other rich and important people. Above all he should not look down on others or neglect the poor and unimportant: they might be rich in other ways. On one occasion some Nepalese pilgrims were reciting mantras while circumambulating one of the temples. Rimpoche had never encountered Nepalese people before, and when he heard their odd pronunciation he burst out laughing. His guru caught hold of him immediately and gave him a sound thrashing. 'Don't you laugh at these people. These Nepalese people are chanting the mantras in the holy Sanskrit language which, as a Tibetan, you can't even get your tongue around!'

Geshe Lhundup lived with Rimpoche in his own household in Loseling College. Each *tulku* had a private *lhabrang* or household, complete with servants, attendants, and a steward who managed the finances. In Loseling, there were over fifty *tulkus* who kept *lhabrangs*, some of which were so large that Geshe Jampel Thardo described them as almost independent countries. Rimpoche's *lhabrang* was not rich, but it was comfortable and quite recognizably the household of an aristocrat. His private study was small but richly decorated. A splendid couch, with a high wooden back painted with dragons and other scenes, was where Rimpoche sat and memorized his texts. Before him on a carved and polished Chinese wooden table was a silver container within which a cylinder filled with mantras was rotated by means of a spindle. Every few minutes Rimpoche would set the mantras spinning whilst silently intoning the syllables with his lips. Each day one of his attendants arranged some foliage in a brilliantly coloured Chinese *cloisonné* vase whose pattern was reflected in the highly polished wooden surface on which it was placed. The walls were lined with patterned cloth and bedecked with finely executed *thangkas*. On the wall behind Rimpoche hung a *thangka* depicting the previous Dhardo Tulku on a splendid throne holding a parchment text in his left hand, while his right was held to his heart where resided the mystic Wheel of the Dharma. When Rimpoche recalled Geshe Lhundup he was deeply moved;

the strength of the bond which had been established at Drepung was apparent.

'I remember my guru with great fondness, and I remember very clearly all his words of advice, kindness, and instruction. In respect of my religious studies he was really a great guru. When I remember and think of those things my eyes well up with tears.'

Much of the time spent with Geshe Lhundup was concerned with instruction in the course of *geshe* studies. He studied a syllabus which had been followed for centuries and which had evolved from that of the great monastic universities of classical Buddhist India. Fifteen subjects were studied in the course of seventeen years. These involved the acquisition of a comprehensive knowledge of the Buddhist sutras, and of the classical texts on the Buddhist Path and the philosophy which accompanies it. In the first class the students were taught to derive, from very simple things, the elements of logical reasoning such as the relationship between the four primary and eight secondary colours. In due course they would apply these principles to profound questions of philosophy.

The emphasis on clear reasoning was reflected in the means through which students were examined. They were set against one another in highly stylized debates in which they contested points of doctrine and interpretation. Points were made and refuted with tremendous emphasis and accompanied by sweeping gestures and hand clapping; rosaries spun as the contestants flew at each other as if life itself depended on it. Advanced students were set particular topics such as knotty points of logic, the exposition of obscure or abstruse passages in the sutras, or the reconciliation of passages from different commentaries. Any false reasoning would be mercilessly exposed by a questioner or an opponent. Occasionally, a new commentary would be written which was clearer than any hitherto published, and a college might use it to replace an old one. If there were inter-college debates by the top students, great excitement was derived from the uncertainty as to which points in a commentary an opponent might use as ammunition, and whether or not the points it made were refutable.

After a grounding in logic, Rimpoche moved on to the study of the mind, the senses, the objects of the senses, and of perception. Here students began to examine the manner in which things appear, and to assess what may and may not be inferred from their appearance. If one is trying to understand the true nature of reality one must not be fooled by assumptions, or tricked by a superficial view of things. The same principles were applied to a variety of other subjects in order to instil a thorough aversion to the bases of false views. Students could then progress to the study of the sutras and their commentaries. These texts, which were composed over a long period, contain many of the most profound and penetrating teachings of Buddhism. Through their study, monks at Drepung gained insights into the paths to Buddhahood which they describe. They studied the different types of realization along the Path, the view of Absolute Reality as propounded by the different Buddhist schools, the practice of the spiritual perfections, and much more.

There was much to absorb, but the students were also Buddhist monks who aspired to put these teachings into practice. Their present task was to imbibe the knowledge which had accumulated over thousands of years and which had been passed down in an uninterrupted lineage. That tradition was the product of strenuous spiritual practice under the inspiration of the Buddha and his Enlightened followers, and it has always stressed that book-knowledge is only a *means* to the attainment of

Insight into the true nature of existence.

The next subject was the principle of *Shunyata*, or 'Emptiness', as seen from the highest viewpoint. A complete understanding of this teaching, tantamount to Enlightenment itself, was the realization of the ineffable nature of all phenomena. This was, understandably, the most demanding section of the course, but its intention was not to produce direct Insight, but to bring about a clear conceptual understanding of the teaching as it had been traditionally expounded. In time, this knowledge would provide the basis on which, after experience of meditative absorption, experience of the reality underlying the teaching might arise.

Ethics and Phenomenology were studied next and they were repeated in the Karam class after which most students graduated as Karampa *geshes*. The top students, however, were selected for the Lharam class and still had several more years to go, during which they studied a further five great treatises.

In addition to these studies, Rimpoche had extra lessons on Tibetan literature, composition, calligraphy, and history. Moreover, four or five years into the *geshe* study course, Geshe Lhundup started to arrange for Rimpoche to attend audiences at which distinguished lamas were giving initiations into meditation practices, or were passing on teachings. Sometimes he was taken for an initiation during breaks in his usual study routine when time was set aside for revision, or he would have to rise earlier in the morning to attend an initiation and catch up on the day's work in the afternoon and evening. Some initiations and teachings took days and weeks to impart, but Geshe Lhundup always made sure that Rimpoche's other work did not suffer.

Throughout the course of his studies, Rimpoche followed an exacting routine. He never found it easy to rise early in the morning, but at 4.00a.m. his guru was always there to wake him.

'While dressing I had to recite "OM A RA PA CA NA DHIH" (the mantra of Manjushri, embodiment of Wisdom). Then I washed my face—during which I had to recite the mantra of Dorje Namjoma (the 'Complete Destroyer'). I then sat on my mat and memorized sutras. After finishing the day's lesson I ate my breakfast and recited the sutras already memorized. I then went to the debating ground where we practise debate and examination. I then took my lunch and, after half an hour's rest, my guru taught me the new lessons that I was to memorize the following day.... In the afternoon I learned more sutras; in the evening I studied the day's lessons till 11p.m. This routine was strictly adhered to throughout the years of my study.'

In spite of the formidable workload and strict discipline at Drepung, one should not imagine that it was a cold or unfriendly place. Rimpoche always demonstrated a strong concern for the people around him:

'I made many friendships with fellow students among the ordinary monks. Some of them were very poor and did not have sufficient food. In spite of these difficulties they paid deep attention to their study. As I had no problems with regard to food myself, I felt very sorry for them, and used to offer them *tsampa* [roast barley-flour] and sometimes money.'

When Rimpoche was eighteen, Geshe Lhundup made his regime tougher still by insisting, in accordance with the strict monastic code, that Rimpoche take only one main meal, at midday. Buddhist monks in south-east Asia follow this practice, but their meal is very large and is preceded by a not inconsiderable breakfast. Rimpoche's breakfast consisted of only a few spoonfuls of *tsampa*. Although Rimpoche lost his evening meal there was no reduction in his work-load, and he still had to memorize, study, and debate until late at night. Often there were all-night debates during which he was examined or would have to examine others; then the next day would continue as normal.

The strain of overwork and undernourishment was too much. He gradually began to suffer from painful stomach upsets, and started losing weight. His normally bright complexion took on a dull pallor. At times, his eyes would dart about and his hands would seek support as dizziness overwhelmed him. After some weeks of this he was so weak and thin that there were serious concerns for his life. The doctors prescribed herbs and potions, *pujas* and mantras, but all to no avail. Finally, one astute doctor explained to Geshe Lhundup that if the boy was to work exceptionally long hours then he must have nourishing and regular food. Geshe Lhundup, already grief-stricken by Rimpoche's condition, admitted that he had been wrong to insist on a single meal and asked Rimpoche's forgiveness for his error. Back on a normal diet his health improved and, henceforth, he always had enough food to give him energy for the long days and the ever more frequent all-night debates.

Special times were allotted on the debating ground in Loseling during which hundreds of monks from each house-division would take turns to practise for debate. Other times were allotted to inter-house debates culminating in the Tsoglang, or pre-examination, involving all twenty-three house-divisions. Here the students who had been studying for some years debated in front of the abbot and collected *geshes* of the college. The subject was the subtle and profound teaching of the Madhyamika, for the

Gelugpas the most important school of Buddhist philosophy, and it was to be the start of Dhardo Rimpoche's
celebrity as a scholar and a debater.

> 'I was able to answer all the difficult questions put by
> several scholars, and must have really impressed the
> assembly with my prompt answers. The learned
> *geshes* were all very appreciative. They were confi-
> dent that I would become a successful *geshe*.'

During the following gala ceremony Rimpoche contracted food poisoning and again prayers had to be conducted for his recovery. After the illness, Geshe Lhundup
started to relax his strictness because 'he thought that I was
delicate.' But Rimpoche was maturing fast and no longer
needed so firm a hand. At the age of eighteen, he came to
a much deeper realization of the need for study, seeing
that without a clear understanding of the path one could
not follow it. He understood too that the mind has many
wrong views which are a hindrance to the arising of
Insight, and that study may correct these views. As
Rimpoche emerged into manhood his spiritual aspirations
began to clarify and to make sense of the course he was
pursuing. The combination of intensive study with the
personal example of his teachers had engendered confidence and humility which, together, formed the basis of
wisdom. In later life, when he was asked about the most
important steps or realizations on his spiritual path, he
recalled an incident from his time at Drepung:

> 'Once when I was attending a religious discourse by
> Kyabje Kangser Dorje Chang what he said made a
> lasting impression upon me. He was talking to many
> Rimpoches, myself included, about the concept of
> *tulkus*.... He said he had been giving teachings for a
> long time and that many disciples always came after-
> wards to make offerings of scarfs and cash. But after

many such teachings a stage had come when he could say to us:

'From now onwards I don't wish to accept your offerings. I have everything I need. I find it meaningless to accumulate all that wealth and to run an estate. I have said this from both the negative and the positive points of view. From the positive point of view, a truly realized Rimpoche is supposed to be empowered to know when he is going to die and where he is going to take rebirth, and so there really is no need for him to make many people run around in order to accumulate wealth. If such a Rimpoche were interested in taking rebirth in a well-to-do family, he could. From the negative point of view: if I were to make my disciples build up an estate for me, what guarantee is there for them that I have the power to direct my rebirth and that I will be able to enjoy the fruit of their labour? In the end there is every possibility that another lucky child, someone else altogether, might inherit it. There really is no justification for giving importance to building an estate.'

Rimpoche commented, 'That was truly a turning point in my life. Even though I was young at the time, what he said has remained deeply embedded in my memory.'

5 Death of a Guru

To be released on account of faintheartedness is useless.
Therefore, don't be afflicted by misery
But rely on a knowledgeable person who has gained the
  meaning of the teaching.
Then even the most difficult will be easily attained.

Therefore, one should not be afraid nor be unhappy
To do what is necessary, but as circumstances should
  warrant,
He should be encouraged by the splendour of the Wise
And go out to attain all those (positive) values.[1]

From the earliest point in Buddhist history there have been monks, and each of the Tibetan schools of Buddhism has a monastic tradition. But the extent to which that tradition is emphasized varies. For instance, in the Nyingmapa tradition it is not at all unusual to find highly venerated *tulkus* who are married. They do not take the saffron robe of the celibate but wear a splendid white robe, bordered with maroon silk brocade—indicating that they are laymen—over their deep red *chubas*. In the fifteenth century, Tsongkhapa had considered that the erosion of the distinction between monks and laymen had led to a faltering sense of the spiritual life as a full-time occupation, and thus to corruption. He reformed the monastic tradition by founding the Gelugpa school in which *tulkus* are invariably monks. They usually take *shramanera*, or novice, ordination at an early age, and abide by a code of thirty-six rules governing their behaviour.

[1] *Jatakamala,* from Guenther, H.V., *Mind in Buddhist Psychology,* Dharma Publishing, Emeryville, USA, 1975

Rimpoche's own *shramanera* ordination was conducted by the thirteenth Dalai Lama when he first came from Dhartsendo at the age of nine. At twenty, novices usually take full ordination, which entails adopting further and more rigorous rules, but Geshe Lhundup advised Rimpoche to spend three more years studying the monastic precepts in order to understand fully the significance of the step he was taking. Finally, in 1941, to Rimpoche's delight, the ceremony was conducted by Kyabje Kangser Dorje Chang. On that occasion there were fifty novices with freshly shaven heads sitting at the head of the five thousand assembled monks of Loseling. Kyabje Kangser Dorje Chang intoned the ceremony from a throne not much lower than the fourteen-foot-high throne of the Dalai Lama, while the preceptors and sponsors assisted the ordinees in the rituals and formalities associated with receiving the robe and the pledging of vows. The fifty novices were divided into little *kulas*, or families, of three or four, each of which undertook the ceremony together. This formed a special bond between them.

The next hurdle was the *geshe* exam. The candidates were assessed in debates. This system has nothing in common with a series of written papers during which the candidate has time to consider how to marshal his knowledge. Instead, candidates gathered in the monastery's debating ground before a high throne on which the abbot sat to judge them. The debates were fiercely demanding, and anything other than an immediate answer meant failure. Finally, the abbot would announce placings and accord grades. Most students graduated with ordinary *geshe* passes, but the top students could continue studying for several more years and graduate as Lharampa *geshes*. Rimpoche passed his exams with distinction, and Geshe Lhundup therefore advised him to sit for the Lharampa class. But although this would be a great honour, and would mean that he might become an important member of the Gelugpa hierarchy, Rimpoche was very worried:

'Personally, I wanted to graduate at ordinary level, because taking a Lharampa *geshe* degree involves much expense. You have to give a big gift to your monastery which might cost 100,000 rupees. [This was equivalent to about £4000.] This put me in a real dilemma. On the one hand there were the demands of the study, and on the other the concern for raising the necessary money. I was so worried I began to lose sleep. At night my heart would pound faster and faster, till I thought I might have a heart attack.'

And so Rimpoche embarked on his final years of study for the Lharampa *geshe* examination, the money being raised eventually through donations and loans. Since the examination was very long, only two students from each college could usually go forward each year. This meant that some students had to wait several years for their turn. It was not until 1944, when he was twenty-six and had completed the course, that Dhardo Rimpoche's name was put forward. Once again he was under enormous pressure. His fame as a debater had spread through his college, through Drepung Monastery, and beyond to other monasteries. He was confident that his knowledge and understanding would secure the top place, but one could never be sure. All it would take was one slip, one hesitation, and he would let down all those who had hoped for so much of him.

Qualifying debates were held during the 1944 New Year Monlam festival. Rimpoche passed these with ease, but then something quite unexpected happened. A brilliant Mongolian, named Shiwalha, unexpectedly put himself forward. He had studied in his home monastery for many years before making the six-month journey to central

Tibet. He had entered Gomang College of Drepung, and had been engaged in the *geshe* studies for many years, so no one had given any thought to when he would make a bid for the *geshe* degree. Rimpoche had often met Shiwalha in debate on the Tsogchon compound, and had great respect for his learning and skill. In the preliminary examinations, Shiwalha also qualified.

The main debates took place at the end of the festival before the assembled monks of all the monasteries in Lhasa, numbering over thirty thousand, in addition to whom there were thousands of visitors. Dhardo Rimpoche and the other students had to undertake three debates in a single day; the final night session lasted several hours. Anyone present might ask a question, and candidates could each expect to face hundreds of questions from the assembled scholars and *geshes*. Once again, any delay meant failure, but Rimpoche answered unhesitatingly, with skill and acumen. Finally he was pitted against Shiwalha, and the two battled it out. Questions were posed and immediately answered until it was obvious that neither could get the better of the other.

Both achieved a Lharampa pass, but the top seven Lharampa students were required to attend further examinations at the Dalai Lama's beautiful summer palace, Norbulingka, before the placings were announced. Even in the absence of the crowds, the atmosphere was far from relaxed. All the highest *geshes* were present, and Shiwalha and Rimpoche were questioned on a vast range of topics. Memory and understanding failed neither; subtle distinctions were offered, proofs substantiated, sutras quoted, and commentaries brought in as support. It was impossible to separate Rimpoche and Shiwalha, but the convention was that if two lamas were judged to be of equal quality, but one was from an outlying region, the higher placing would always be granted to the foreigner, to encourage others to make the dangerous journey to Lhasa. Geshe Lhundup had found himself in the same position and, like him, Dhardo Rimpoche was awarded second place while the Mongolian Shiwalha took the first. Lhundup was delighted with his student, and all agreed that the debate had been outstanding.

Dhardo Rimpoche's success in the *geshe* exams represented a triumphant mastery of Buddhism as a body of doctrines. But these doctrines are merely the bones beneath the flesh of Buddhist practice. At the heart of Tibetan Buddhism are the meditational rituals of the Vajrayana, or Tantra, which are no less complex and extensive than the doctrines studied in the *geshe* course. The *geshes* who had been awarded a Lharampa placement were seen as the men to whom the accumulated experience of the Gelugpas might be entrusted and who would pass that experience on to future generations. They were now expected to master Vajrayana practices by attending one of the two Tantric colleges in Lhasa, Gyu-med or Gyo-to, where they were taught by the most accomplished Gelugpa lamas. Students received initiations and empowerments in the course of highly elaborate rituals, and were required to study every aspect of the accompanying music, liturgy, symbolic gesture, and so on. There were empowerments which transmit the spirit necessary to take up the meditations on particular Buddhas and Bodhisattvas; there were rituals authorizing the student to give permission for the study and practice of certain teachings; and there were rituals in which a revered master bestowed his blessing from a state of meditative equipoise. Authorizations and initiations were accompanied by well-defined commitments to practise the ritual which had been imparted. Solitary retreats lasting for months or even years were sometimes required before one was qualified to pass some of these practices on. Within a few months, Rimpoche had received initiations which gave him permission to practise literally hundreds of meditations.

Conditions at the college were very basic. Food was minimal in both quantity and quality; there was no heating, but shoes were not permitted and the monks went barefoot through summer and winter. They still lay down to sleep at 11.00p.m. but now rose at 2.30a.m. and, during sleep, neither head nor feet were to be shown. Since blankets were not allowed, the only way to accomplish this was to sleep sitting upright, wrapped in the monastic robe. Most new students found this pattern of life very difficult, and Rimpoche was no exception. He was used to eating nutritious food, especially during the eight years since his illness, and he struggled with the cold and lack of sleep. These conditions began to tell on his health.

But although it was very hard, Rimpoche took his commitments very seriously. Many monks were senior to him, but within a few months he was awarded fifth place in an examination taken only by the Lharamapa *geshes* of the college. Passing this would enable him to progress towards the pinnacle of the Gelugpa hierarchy, the post of Ganden Tripa.

One day, news came from Lhasa that Geshe Lhundup was sick. Rimpoche rushed to see him and tended him personally. Doctors were called and *pujas* performed, but it was obvious that he was dying. He told Rimpoche that he had long had a strong impression that he had one major task in his life, the education of Dhardo Tulku. This was now complete and he felt satisfied that he could die. He wanted to visit the celestial realm of Tushitaloka in order to sit at the feet of the ancient Indian sages, Atisha and Maitreya, who were reputed to be teaching there. 'Geshela' had a final meeting with each of his disciples and offered them parting advice and instructions. Then, after just a few days of illness, he died peacefully.

An almost unbearable sadness sank to the bottom of Dhardo Rimpoche's heart. The strain of prolonged study, the tremendous expectations he had been subject to, the burden of uncertain finances, and the harsh conditions at Gyu-med College, were too much. His health broke down completely. He suffered from sickness, headaches, and dizziness, and he lost weight. Doctors were brought to him but no cure could be found. Rimpoche himself sought out many physicians but they could do nothing. Finally, he had no option but to withdraw from Tantric college. In doing so he gave up progress on the path which led to the post of Ganden Tripa, the 'Joyous Throne Holder', which some of his junior class-mates were later to attain.

6 Out of the Snows

This morning in the house of Heaven,
We opened the cloud gate,
Rode the sun's rays, and came.
This evening we are bound for India
To attend the sacramental feast
In Cool Garden Cemetery.[1]

Rimpoche was desperate to find a cure, and the only apparent solution was to seek medical help outside Tibet. So in the summer of 1947, when he was twenty-nine, he made the trip to India with his father and five or six attendants. Of all the routes in and out of Tibet, the one he followed, from Lhasa to Kalimpong, was one of the busiest, and perhaps the safest, but there were dangers enough. Some of the passes were 16,000 feet high and blizzards could suddenly descend upon an unsuspecting traveller. There were gorges traversed only by precarious bridges of rope supporting lines of single planks; there were mountain tracks so narrow that a single wrong step could plunge one thousands of feet to one's death; and, strange to say, there were steamy jungles infested with blood-sucking leeches and mosquitoes which infected travellers with tropical diseases. The journey was arduous even for those in the best of health, but Rimpoche was consumed with deep grief at the loss of his teacher and by sadness at not having been able to complete his studies. Oblivious of the terrain, he was looking ahead to India where he hoped he might find a Western doctor who could

[1] *The Hundred Thousand Songs of Milarepa*, trans. Garma C.C. Chang, Shambala, Boulder and London, 1977

offer a cure.

Very few high-ranking lamas had come out of Tibet before Dhardo Rimpoche. A few had made short trips to the Buddhist pilgrimage sites on the plains, but they had been unable to bear the heat, and had hurried back to the cooler climate of the Himalayas. All along Rimpoche's route across the mountains people came to meet him and asked for his blessing. In Kalimpong, where the trade route ended, he was given a rapturous greeting by the Tibetan community.

Kalimpong sprawls along the top of a four-thousand-foot-high ridge at the eastern end of the Himalayas, only a few miles from Bhutan. Like Dhartsendo, it was a trading town where middle-men grew rich. The bazaar was bustling with all the peoples of the eastern Himalayas— Gurkhas, Tamangs, Lepchas, Newaris, Sherpas, Bhutias, Sikkimese—as well as Tibetan and Mongolian traders. Like the Chinese traders who were unwilling to ascend into freezing and lonely Tibet and would stop in Dhartsendo, Tibetans and Mongolians would stop at Kalimpong, unwilling to descend to the bustling furnace of India. But Kalimpong was dominated by the British, who had cultivated it as a 'hill-station', a refuge from the heat. It had been annexed from Bhutan in the 1860s, but Rimpoche arrived during the last days of the Raj. There were majors, colonels, captains, and army wives—fugitives from the stifling plains. There were missionaries attempting to deliver the land from 'error's claim' and the heathen from his folly. And the British had brought their servants: turbaned Sikhs bearing silver trays, swarthy Mahar *dobhis*, Gujerati cooks, and Bengali clerks.

Rimpoche was recommended a doctor in the neighbouring town of Darjeeling, and his health gradually improved. His stomach settled, the headaches and dizziness became less severe, and he started to gain weight. One

1. Thangka of Dhardo Tulku, *1834-1918*

2. Dorje Drak Gompa in Dhartsendo, *1947*

5. Opposite: Rimpoche's guru – Geshe Yeshe Lhundup, Lhasa, *late 1930s*

3. Dhardo Rimpoche's mother, *1950s*

4. Rimpoche, aged 19, in his study at Drepung

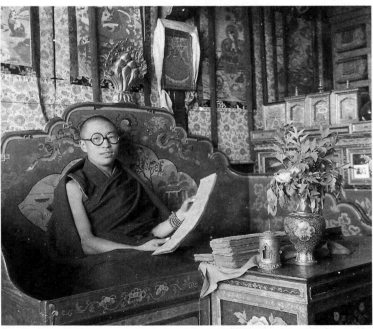

6. Rimpoche with
Sikkimese royal family,
Bodh Gaya, *1956*
front: Princess
Coocoo-la, Rustamji's
mother, Diwan
Rustamji, Rimpoche,
Maharaja of Sikkim
rear: Lobsang
Lhalungpa and Berniak
Kazi (Maharaja's
private secretary)

7. Rimpoche at Yi Ga
Choling in Ghoom,
late 1950s

afternoon the doctor gave him some medicine and told him to stay in bed, but while the doctor was sitting outside in the sunshine, Rimpoche started to think of all the trouble he was causing. He thought of the two attendants who were currently looking after him, and thought too how worried his mother must be. It struck him forcibly that he should not be the source of so much disturbance, so he got up and went outside into the garden. The doctor was alarmed, but Rimpoche told him that he would only have a few minutes in the sun and then go back to bed. Back in his room he felt a calm and ease of mind which he had rarely experienced in the past months; so he performed a *puja* and meditated. For the next few days he did the same thing, and quite soon felt completely cured. For a few years he occasionally experienced headaches and dizziness, but he was now restored to fitness. Good health was not to desert him until he was over seventy.

After a month in Kalimpong, Rimpoche decided to make a pilgrimage to the Buddhist holy places. With his two attendants he set out for the plains of India to visit places which had hitherto possessed a semi-mythical reality for him through their appearances in the sutras. He visited Bodh Gaya, where the Buddha attained Enlightenment, Sarnath where he had delivered his first teaching, Rajagriha where many later teachings had been given, and he visited the remains of the great monastic university of Nalanda. On his return to Kalimpong, A.P. Sherpa, with whom he was staying, asked him to take the opportunity to give teachings and initiations, so Rimpoche gave a series of teachings on *Lam-Rim*, or 'the Stages of the Path', over a period of several months. The people of Kalimpong and the surrounding localities who crowded into A.P. Sherpa's house were delighted by Rimpoche's teaching. He was clear and practical but, at the same time, he was learned; he was young, had an agile mind, and he was accessible.

Above all, he did not stand on ceremony. Some people wanted blessings while others asked for special initiations, especially the long-life meditations of Amitayus, Tara, and Ushnishavijaya. Whenever Rimpoche spoke of returning to Tibet, his new disciples would plead with him to stay, and he remained in the district for over eight months.

Eventually Rimpoche made the return journey to Lhasa, where he wished to resume his studies, and lost no time in attending more teachings and empowerments. He undertook the teaching work which was expected of a *geshe* and he was made the tutor of two important *tulkus*, Didruk Rimpoche, a *tulku* of a previous regent, and Trangpa Tritul Rimpoche, a *tulku* of a previous Ganden Tripa. But at the beginning of 1949, when he had only been back in Lhasa for eighteen months, other events were to change the course of his life dramatically.

A lama from the little kingdom of Ladakh, called Ngawang Samten, had formed the idea of building a Tibetan temple at Bodh Gaya. At first he had only been able to erect a few small buildings, but he approached the Tibetan government for support and was eventually able to raise enough money to build a small temple. In 1947 he went on a two-year fund-raising tour. While he was gone, another monk took charge. That monk fell sick and died, and his place was taken by one Amdo Kelsang. When Ngawang Samten returned the two fell out and, as misunderstandings multiplied, he decided to present the monastery to the Tibetan government. Having heard something of Dhardo Rimpoche's success in India, he requested that he should be sent to be the new abbot. The Tibetan government seems to have had the impression that this was quite a substantial temple (although there were only two or three monks there at the time) and the regent, Taktra Rimpoche, decided to comply. Rimpoche was part way through an important retreat when he was summoned by the regent and told that he was being sent to Bodh Gaya. He politely, but firmly, refused. But Taktra Rimpoche told him that it had been decided that he would be abbot and that he must go; Rimpoche said that if this was the case he would go after his studies were completed, and only for a few years. But the regent insisted: 'No. You just go.' Mochok Rimpoche, one of Rimpoche's teachers, after performing a ritual divination, counselled him 'It is better you go now or next year. After then you will not be able to go.'

A few months later Rimpoche made the journey to India, accompanied by his mother, his steward, his main attendant, and a few servants, while several mules and ponies carried their luggage. This consisted mainly of texts; there were selections from the works of previous Dalai Lamas, the collected works of other important teachers, the basic texts of Mahayana Buddhism with their Tibetan commentaries, and there were several volumes concerning initiations and rituals which Rimpoche might have to perform. Rimpoche considered it a small selection, but in the hard times ahead his library would be the only one left containing a number of essential texts.

Rimpoche travelled, along with his attendant, to Bodh Gaya, which he had thought never to see again. The new *gompa* was much smaller than the government had believed, but, small as it was, this was where he would spend much of the next twelve years.

7 By the Diamond Throne

Bodh Gaya! Bodh Gaya! How many people have come to
you in the course of ages! How many pilgrim feet have
trodden the dust of your groves, how many pairs of hands
been joined in silent adoration beneath the wide-spreading
boughs of the Tree of Enlightenment, how many heads
touched in profound thanksgiving the edge of the
Diamond Throne! Bodh Gaya! Bodh Gaya! How beautiful
you are in the morning, with the sunlight streaming on
the renovated façade of your great temple as it rises four-
square against the cloudless blue sky! How beautiful you
are in the evening, when in the shadowy depths of the
deserted temple courtyard a thousand votive lamps glitter
like reflections of the stars! Bodh Gaya, I shall always
remember how beautiful you were the first time I saw
you, when my heart was young, and you made me your
own![1]

Bodh Gaya is a place to inspire the heart and soul of the
sensitive Buddhist. Sangharakshita, a young English-born
Buddhist monk, wrote these words, recalling his first visit
to Bodh Gaya in 1949. But while there was much to inspire
a pilgrim, there was also much to disturb. In the middle of
the shrine which marks the spot where the Buddha gained
Enlightenment, was a stone lingam, or phallic symbol, of
the Hindu god Shiva. Buddhists were not considered fit to
conduct the worship, and Hindu Brahmins insisted on
doing so 'for a consideration'.

On his arrival at the Tibetan temple, Dhardo Rimpoche
found that the earlier misunderstandings had left a legacy

[1] from *The Thousand-Petalled Lotus*

of bitterness within the monastery, whilst Amdo Kelsang was now ensconced in a position of power which he was unwilling to relinquish. Rimpoche had arrived with two officers appointed by the Tibetan government and with papers bearing the regent's seal confirming his appointment as *khenpo*, or abbot. But Amdo Kelsang strenuously questioned these credentials, never having seen a Tibetan governmental seal before, and he was supported by some of the other monks. Rimpoche and his officers decided they would have to compromise and, in return for the monks' agreement to Rimpoche's installation as *khenpo*, Amdo Kelsang was allowed to retain an important position in the *gompa*. Thus, from the outset, the tiny monastery contained rival factions; the older inhabitants were opposed to Dhardo Rimpoche's regime almost as a matter of course.

Because Bodh Gaya was an important place for all denominations of Buddhists, Rimpoche came into contact with the Buddhist world beyond Tibet. 'One day while I was looking through the window of my room, I saw an English person in yellow monastic robes on the roof of the Maha Bodhi Society's rest house.... I was quite astonished and intrigued that a Westerner should be interested in our religion.' So surprised was he that he even called his attendant to come and see the monk. 'Now the Dharma has gone even as far as the West!' he announced.

The *gompa* was in need of drastic reform. No accounts had ever been kept and, although it received quite substantial donations, the monks had only spent enough on the temple to cover its bare running costs while splitting the rest between themselves. This meant that the *gompa* had no toilet facilities, no water, and nothing had been set aside for renovation and improvements. The resident monks had been happy with this meagre subsistence, but they were oblivious of the needs of the increasing numbers of Tibetan pilgrims who crowded around it. To Sangharakshita these pilgrims were a great inspiration:

> 'They were poor, they were ragged, they were dirty, and the other pilgrims looked down on them, but they had walked all the way from Tibet, some of them with babies on their backs, and now they came shuffling in through the gate with their prayer-wheels and rosaries in their hands and expressions of ecstacy on their upturned faces. For them, history did not exist.... They did not even see the brahmins. As they circumambulated the temple, as they prostrated themselves before the Diamond Throne, as they lit butter-lamps round the Bodhi tree, they saw only the naked fact of the Buddha's Supreme Enlightenment, and through their eyes, even if not with my own, I could see it too.'

Rimpoche, one may assume, felt the presence of the Buddha for himself, and when he looked at the pilgrims he felt his responsibilities in the face of their dirt and rags. Most arrived with virtually no money and had nowhere to stay, so Rimpoche often let them erect a piece of canvas by the *gompa* to offer a scant covering while they slept. Sometimes he would give them food or money, but there was hardly any money to give; their poverty was matched by that of the monastery, and the problem lay with the monks. Rimpoche insisted that proper accounts be kept and that each monk be given a regular, but fixed, sum for his support. The rest of the *gompa's* income was put into a communal fund which might rapidly accumulate. Rimpoche hoped that, on this basis, he could build the temple that the pilgrims needed and of which he could be proud.

Rimpoche gathered the monks together and announced that he planned to build a *dharamsala,* or rest house, for the pilgrims. They responded with gales of derision until they saw that he was quite serious. Some of the monks still resented their reduced income and were jealous of their dwindling power. The monastery was filled with whispering. Dhardo Rimpoche, they said, was an upstart who was trying to make a name for himself; his plan was foolish and it would ruin the *gompa*. While he was at Drepung Rimpoche had been ordained as a novice Bodhisattva, and one of his vows stated that it was an offence 'not to take steps to put an end to slanders about oneself'. He gathered the monks once again and spoke forthrightly. 'Building a rest house' he said 'is essential, not only to welcome the pilgrims in a befitting manner, but also to encourage more to come—which, in turn, will mean greater support for the temple and make more resources available.'

In 1950, as building work was about to start on the *dharamsala*, Rimpoche conducted a ceremony exorcizing evil forces and invoking the protectors. He had planned a *dharamsala* which would house fifty pilgrims. He often spent the whole day on the site supervising the local workers, or even joined in the labouring work himself. A long period in which Rimpoche had been unsure of his direction was coming to an end. 'Because of the busy and heavy work schedule', he said, 'my illness vanished and the headaches cleared completely. I felt that because of my coming out of Tibet and working so hard I had a new lease of life.' His plans now extended beyond the new *dharamsala*; he envisaged a monastery which could house over forty monks. A well was sunk in the grounds to give a regular supply of water and, risking further disparagement, Rimpoche rebuilt the pitiful hut which had comprised the abbot's quarters in a form more appropriate to the office. By 1953, the work was completed.

The monastery was physically improved and financially sound, but its internal divisions were not at an end.

More monks joined, arriving from different monasteries from across Tibet, and tried to adapt themselves to working with one another under Dhardo Rimpoche. At Drepung, Geshe Yeshe Lhundup had always impressed upon him the importance of adhering to the monastic code and, now that he was abbot of his own monastery, he was determined to run it in accordance with these ancient rules. The purpose of many of these had long since been forgotten and others had come to be neglected or ignored, but Rimpoche took infinite pains to consult their canonical sources in order to understand how and why they had been instituted and how they might be interpreted in a manner which was in keeping with their spirit. But he insisted that those under him follow a strict regime. Geshe Jampel Thardo recalled that 'Rimpoche was always checking on the rules of the monastery: what *pujas* they did, what practices, and so forth'. In the face of this 'the monks were not easy'. Most were over thirty and had been used to varying degrees of strictness; they found it difficult to repose trust in a young man of whom they knew little. Moreover, Rimpoche could be very outspoken and the monastery was very small. In a frank discussion he told me, 'The main thing is that I was a strict disciplinarian and used to keep things under very strict control, which many of them disliked.'

Soon, however, events in Tibet overshadowed the difficulties that Rimpoche was experiencing at Bodh Gaya, and highlighted the importance of what he had managed to establish. Before his departure many anxious glances had been cast towards China, where the forces of Mao Tse Tung appeared to be advancing towards victory. China had been so long threatening and so long divided that the people expected, and the lamas hoped, that the Communists would be kept occupied in fighting the Nationalist forces of Chang Kai Check. But in 1949 troublesome portents appeared in the heavens and the People's Liberation Army massed on Tibet's eastern border. A wave of fear swept the country. The government ordered the monasteries to hold rituals invoking propitiatory forces and the diplomats to seek the assistance of foreign powers. Desperate and then despairing appeals were made to Britain, America, India, and Nepal, but none would speak in Tibet's defence. She had neglected to join the United Nations, and her plea for its assistance was disregarded; India had itself only recently emerged into independence, and advised Tibet to placate their common enemy. Negotiations took place in Delhi in 1950 but, while the diplomats talked, the People's Liberation Army marched into eastern Tibet, outflanked and captured the small Tibetan army, and gained control of Chamdo Province.

Marxism and the Chinese revolution seemed to belong to a world entirely different from that inhabited by the monks of Tibet. They had striven to remain isolated even from the pervasive, but relatively benign, influence of the West. But some had had harsh experience of Communism at first hand. Geshe Wangyal, one of Rimpoche's friends from Drepung, had been a pupil of Dorjieff, the powerful Buryat monk who had been tutor to the thirteenth Dalai Lama. When he was nineteen, Wangyal had worked with Dorjieff in St Petersburg. When Wangyal had returned to Tibet, Dorjieff had stayed in Russia after the Revolution and had continued to teach the Dharma until his activities were suppressed by Stalin. Wangyal was able to gather that his teacher had been imprisoned, had probably been tortured, and that he had died in 1941. Meanwhile, in the thirties, Wangyal had personally witnessed the obliteration of Buddhism in Mongolia, and it seemed to him that the establishment of Communist rule meant nothing less that the eradication of the Dharma. At the first sign of an invasion by Chinese Communists, he had left Tibet for India. Rimpoche, with whom Wangyal had spoken, followed the progress of the Chinese armies in the Indian press. The news of the invasion affected him deeply.

In late 1950, as the Communist forces were nearing Lhasa, the regent resigned in favour of the sixteen-year-old Dalai Lama, who immediately moved the government to Yatung near the Sikkimese border. Five months later they returned to Lhasa, but many government officials sent their families and their belongings to India for safety. In Darjeeling and Kalimpong they formed what was recognizably a first, though small, aristocratic wave of refugees. Meanwhile, the Chinese Army had marched into Lhasa, and their number steadily increased until there were almost ten thousand troops in the city. Within a few months, Lhasa had changed beyond all recognition. While famine spread through the streets, the Communists instituted daily 're-education' programmes and political science classes; they formed 'patriotic' associations and commandeered houses, land, and estates. Old Tibet was dying, its political independence had effectively been lost, and the guardians of its culture and religion braced themselves for a further onslaught.

When the government moved to the border, Rimpoche travelled up through Sikkim to offer his support and advice. Yatung was crowded out. The local Gelugpa monastery was full of monk-officials and the best houses lodged aristocratic families who were involved in government business. Rimpoche had to take lodgings with an ordinary family in the town and, since he was abbot of the *gompa* at Bodh Gaya, had to go to the makeshift offices time and again concerning official work. It was against the background of these circumstances that Rimpoche received a teaching from a quite unexpected quarter. In his own words:

'When I reached my lodging I found the doors were open, and so, not being sure if anyone was in or not I called out "Hui! Hui! Is anybody in?" Since there was no reply I went upstairs, but when I went into the kitchen I saw the old *Pala* [*lit.* grandfather] sitting in the corner. He was on old man with a defect in one of his eyes. I exclaimed "O Pala, You are here!" and then told him, "As for me I could not go to the offices because all the people had gone to teachings by Trijang Rimpoche [Senior Tutor to the Dalai Lama], and I could not go to the teachings because one cannot arrive in the middle. Also, I've been going to the offices for the past several days and today I thought of coming down and having a little rest."...
So I asked him where the other members of the family had gone. The old man replied, "Oh the other members of my family have gone to temper their minds!" I was really intrigued and puzzled by what he said: "Temper the mind."—That really set me thinking. But since I did not really understand the full importance of what he had said we started talking about other things. Then, afterwards, I asked him again whether the other members of the family had gone to the hills or the forest to collect firewood, or something. The old man said, "Oh Rimpoche! I spoke to you in a riddle and you didn't understand me! Rimpoche, the members of my family have all gone to the religious teaching, and that's why I said that they had gone to temper their minds. And the reason is that in the past, in our town, we did not have any lamas to give teachings, nor were there Rimpoche's that we could go to. Yet, in spite of that, the people of the town, who were actually very poor, were quite a happy lot, very friendly with each other, very helpful. They shared their sorrows and joys with each other.

But later on, as lamas and Rimpoches started coming
to give teachings, I began to notice that the people
had changed from being friendly and cooperative to
being more aggressive and individualistic, more
worldly-minded. So the people were not taming their
minds in spite of the teachings—they were getting
worse and worse! That is why I said to you that they
had gone to temper, sharpen, hone, their minds." So
when the old man said this so directly, so openly, to
me, a Rimpoche, it sent shivers through me. The
meeting with the old man was a very important
incident in my life.'

Through this lesson Rimpoche began to see another side
of Tibetan Buddhism—a side which worked contrary to
the purpose of the Dharma. He could see through the eyes
of the old man how a community could lose its unity when
people ceased to relate to each other, and grabbed hungri-
ly at the latest and highest teachings offered by the established heirarchy. Such reflections in no way diminished
his respect for the great lamas of Tibet, but radically challenged his views on how the Dharma should be taught.

After the Dalai Lama's government had returned to
Lhasa more Tibetans moved to India, including many
from the merchant class and the richer monk-officials.
Rimpoche realized that he would never return to Tibet and
bitterly regretted not having the opportunity to complete
his studies; the conditions which might have allowed this
no longer obtained. From now on he would make his
home in India and work there for the preservation of the
Dharma, and, in this light, his work for the Bodh Gaya
gompa seemed to take on a new significance. Following the
invasion of Tibet, it seemed likely that the light of the
Dharma would be extinguished in his homeland; if it was
to continue to burn, it would henceforth burn in exile.

8   Prayer Flags in the Wind

May the beings who contribute to the creation
of Images of Maitreya, the Buddha of Love,
Experience the Dharma of the Great Way
In the presence of Maitreya himself.

When like a sun rising from behind the mountain,
The Buddha of Love appears at the Diamond seat,
May the lotus of wisdom be opened
And the Living beings swarm to drink truth's honey.[1]

In India the hot season lasts from March to June. Vegetation is burnt to a crisp, rivers and wells run dry, and, in the villages, huddles of peasants are to be seen digging in dried-up water courses. Tibetans find the heat of the plains unbearable, and most of them retreat to the coolness of the Himalayan foothills. Every year, Dhardo Rimpoche left Bodh Gaya during the hot season for a small house which he had rented for his mother and her attendants in Tir-pai, on the outskirts of Kalimpong. The scholar, Rene de Nebesky-Wojkowitz, spent a great deal of time with Rimpoche in 1951–2 and devoted a chapter to him in his memoirs, *Where the Gods are Mountains,* in which he describes how 'Dando Tulku' (as he calls him) lived in Kalimpong:

> 'Dando tulku lived ... in the house of a Tibetan merchant situated on the mountain ridge above the Tibetan quarter.... The spacious house-chapel on the first floor had been arranged as a living-room for him. Next to the great altar stood the *tulku's* throne—a

[1] A Prayer to Maitreya, from Glenn H. Mullin, *Selected Works of the Dalai Lama I,* Snow Lion, New York, 1985

high seat made from a pile of cushions covered with costly brocade. In front of him on the seat stood a low, richly carved little table with ritual implements and books on it. Above the saint's head was draped a dark red canopy, and the wall behind the seat was covered with costly painted scrolls that were changed according to the nature of the ceremony the Rimpoche was carrying out on any particular day.'

Rimpoche's personal attendant was Lobsang Namkha. He was the son of the steward of Jampa Rimpoche's estate in Dhartsendo and, as boys, he and Dhardo Rimpoche had together made their formal pledges as Buddhists to Jampa Rimpoche. Later, when Dhardo Rimpoche was studying at Drepung, Lobsang had been sent there too. The cousin of Jampa Rimpoche with whom he had been staying intended to return to Dhartsendo, taking Lobsang with him. At the last minute Lobsang fell sick and had to be left behind, and since Lobsang was very poor, Rimpoche offered to take him into his own *lhabrang* as a servant. He proved capable and devoted, was scrupulously upright, and could be trusted with money. Soon they became close friends and, when Rimpoche went to India, Lobsang accompanied him and remained with him until he died a few years before his master. Throughout those years Lobsang was a constant presence, silently preparing butter-lamps, setting out ritual implements, or painting a mandala for one of Rimpoche's ceremonies. 'He was like a right hand,' Rimpoche told me, 'and closer than a brother.'

Rimpoche's mother also figures prominently in Nebesky-Wojkowitz's account of the household:

'She was a nice old lady who tirelessly let the beads of her rosary slip between her fingers. She usually wore a dark brown chuba gathered with a broad yellow silk sash. Her head was shaven, as is customary for nuns of the Yellow Hat [Gelugpa] sect. It was a very good thing that her firm hand was there to run the household and the servants, for Rimpoche was completely absorbed in his religious studies and meditations.'

The 'firm hand' even extended to ensuring that her son was given the respect due to a *tulku*. If any visitors brought offering-gifts of insufficient value, they would be sent packing with the words, "My son's not an ordinary lama. He's a high *tulku*, you know!" This was entirely against Rimpoche's wishes—he was delighted to meet anybody who came to visit him, with or without a gift. Eventually, Rimpoche sent his mother on a long pilgrimage to the sacred places, and, much to her chagrin, on her return had the servants and household firmly in his own hands. Over the years she was to prove quite a challenge to Rimpoche, since she became quite angry and bitter, and complained over her displacement to anyone willing to listen.

Nebesky-Wojkowitz was researching Tibetan Buddhist iconography and availed himself of Rimpoche's help. Rimpoche agreed to give him tuition in Tibetan and, in return, Nebesky-Wojkowitz helped Rimpoche in his attempts to learn English.

'When I first came into the chapel to teach Rimpoche I wondered how these lessons were going to be carried out. Up to now we had sat opposite one another—the Rimpoche up on his throne, I on one of the visitors' cushions with the interpreter beside me. This time, the Rimpoche came down from his elevated seat, pulled up a low table, and sat down beside me with crossed legs, laughing unconcernedly—to the utter stupefaction of his servants, who doubtless saw in this a serious breach of Tibetan etiquette.'

Nebesky-Wojkowitz also observed the honour which the

community accorded their newly resident *tulku*. This was so great that 'every evening, crowds of Tibetans marched round the Rimpoche's house muttering prayers'; in the streets 'people came running up from all sides. They jostled one another to touch the Rimpoche's robe with their foreheads as they bowed reverently, while women pushed their children forward to be blessed, which the Rimpoche did by the usual laying on of hands.' Some years later, though many other important lamas had now passed through Kalimpong, the Tibetan community's affection for Rimpoche had hardly diminished. Sangharakshita remembers that, at times, it was hard for Rimpoche to make his way from one end of the high street to the other.

Among the ordinary people of the Tibetan community there was always a great demand for Rimpoche to make predictions of one sort or another. In Tibet, he had received initiations into the meditations and rituals of a mysterious protectress, Palden Lamo, 'The Glorious Goddess', which, it is said, bless one with powers of divination. Nebesky-Wojkowitz witnessed several such scenes; the petitioner made the traditional threefold obeisance and then offered a scarf containing a coin as a token of payment.

'One man wanted to know what demonic influences were responsible for the sudden illness of his son, what should be done to cure the child and whether he would survive the sickness ... and a woman enquired how the members of her family who had stayed behind in Lhasa were faring.'

At such times Rimpoche would take out a little silver pot which contained three dice. With eyes screwed tightly closed he would silently invoke Palden Lamo with her mantra, hold the dice to his forehead, and let them fall before him. Rimpoche visualized himself as Palden Lamo and blew on the dice, not for good luck, but in order to bless the dice with Palden Lamo's breath. Consulting the meditation text, Rimpoche would interpret the answer in accordance with the question asked. It was usual for his predictions to be very accurate. As the supplicant left, 'sometimes he took one of the narrow silk ribbons lying ready at his side, breathed on it, and then placed it round his visitor's neck as a talisman.'

Sometimes, wealthy Tibetan merchants sponsored Rimpoche to impart initiations and public teachings. They ensured that the correct offerings were made and that there was a plentiful supply of food and butter tea. On such occasions Rimpoche's throne would be carried outside and placed under a huge, ceremonial, yellow parasol. Rimpoche himself would appear in formal dress—a rich, wine-red upper and lower robe, with a brocade underjacket bordered with red and trimmed with fine blue cord. Hanging from his waist was a *chablu*, a sort of large, flat, water-flask carried in a square of silk brocade embroidered with a Chinese dragon. On his feet he wore thick, white felt boots, embellished with blue and yellow patterns and upturned soles. While teaching, he would wear a bright yellow, patched, cotton upper robe, and a tall, pointed, yellow *pandit* cap, lined with gold and embroidered with flowers in crimson silk thread.

In 1951, Rimpoche was requested to become *khenpo* or abbot of the famous Yi Ga Choling Monastery, some three hours journey from Kalimpong. It was a small monastery situated in the little village of Ghoom on the misty heights of a 7,500ft mountain spur—at the highest point on the journey from the plains to Darjeeling. As a traveller ascends the path leading to the monastery he passes rows of poles from which stream long lines of cotton prayer flags. These vibrate constantly in the wind, and drone as they do so with a low, singing hum. If he is fortunate he may catch, through the mist, a first sight of the spectacular

Kangchenjunga range of the Himalayas. This was the year Sangharakshita made a visit to Ghoom with his friend, the German Buddhist, Lama Anagarika Govinda:

> 'There was mist everywhere. The name Ghoom was indeed said to mean mist or fog, and it was well known that however clear a day it might be down at Tista Bridge or in Darjeeling, on passing through Ghoom one would be sure to encounter anything from a thick blanket of white cloud, through which the grey-blue shapes of the pines loomed like the shadows of giants, to a veil of mist so fine as to be almost invisible.'[1]

But Rimpoche had so much work to do on the building project at Bodh Gaya, and on bringing together its monastic community, that he had little inclination to take on a further commitment. The monks of Yi Ga Choling realized that Rimpoche could never be a full-time abbot, but it was more important to them to have a well-qualified lama with some degree of spirituality than a good full-time administrator. Although sympathetic, Rimpoche felt he could not do justice to the monastery or to the resident monks and, reluctantly, declined the offer. But the monks were determined. The mother of the young Dalai Lama (who was known as 'the Great Mother' and was a woman of some influence) had fallen sick while visiting Darjeeling, and Rimpoche had been called to conduct pujas for her health. The monks approached her and requested that she make an entreaty on their behalf. Promising to do all she could, she presented the request in such a forceful manner that Rimpoche could not refuse.

The monastery had been founded by a Mongolian lama in 1850 and was reputed to be the oldest Tibetan temple in

---

[1] *FWBO Newsletter* No. 66, Summer 1985

India. In *The Way of the White Clouds* Lama Govinda describes how he was caught in a fierce storm and given refuge at Yi Ga Choling while on his way back to Ceylon from an International Buddhist Conference in Darjeeling in the early 1930s:

'The monastery itself, situated on a mountain-spur jutting out high above the deep valleys ... seemed to be tossed about in a cauldron of boiling clouds, rising up from the invisible dark valleys, lit up only by continual lightning, while other clouds seemed to be sweeping down from the icy ranges of the central Himalayas ... adding to the confusion of the elements. The uninterrupted rumble of thunder, the deafening noise of hail on the roof, and the howling of the storm filled the air.'

At the time, the great visionary lama, Tomo Geshe Rimpoche, was living in retreat in the gompa. Many years before he had beheld a vision of Maitreya Buddha, the Buddha of Friendliness (who, it is believed, will be the teacher of future ages) and had been inspired to erect statues of Maitreya all over Tibet. He built an especially beautiful one in the meditation hall at Yi Ga Choling. That statue is still there, and still in perfect condition; Maitreya seems to radiate a gentle, golden light which reaches to the furthest corners of the darkness; his bejewelled head towers high and his eyes gaze serenely as if in contemplation of an inner truth. People come from far and near to pay homage to the 'Future Buddha', touching their foreheads in adoration on the golden toes of the statue, leaving a few coins in token of their gratitude. The walls have been cracked by the upheavals of several earthquakes and their frescoes are now barely visible beneath a layer of soot, but when Govinda saw them they were very different:

'There were many-armed monsters embracing each

other in sexual union, surrounded by flames and smoke, and, close to them, enhaloed saints serenely resting on lotus flowers, with devotees at their feet. There were fairies of tender beauty and fierce goddesses in ecstatic dance, adorned with skulls and garlands of human heads, while ascetics were absorbed in meditation and scholars in teaching their disciples.'

Day by day and week by week, the golden figure and the frescoed walls worked their magic upon Govinda. Slowly, the dry crust of his life as a Theravada *bhikkhu* crumbled to reveal a soul which had been starved of the nourishment of colour and myth. Govinda watched the temple attendant as he performed his round of ritual devotions, noting that he seemed to be lit by a light from within, akin to the radiance of the golden statue. Such heartfelt devotion, even to this strange pantheon of figures, seemed truer to the spirit of the Buddha's teaching than the lifeless approach of Theravada Buddhism. No less profound was his meeting with Tomo Geshe Rimpoche, under whose influence Govinda slowly gained entry to the world of Tibetan Buddhism. Through *The Way of the White Clouds* Yi Ga Choling Gompa has since become known the world over as an archetypal Tibetan monastery.

Rimpoche found that his duties at the monastery were, in some ways, far more agreeable than those at Bodh Gaya. There was no friction between himself and the monks who were, in general, older, more used to discipline, and able to work together. They were also unstinting in their devotion to Rimpoche. The abbot's quarters consisted of just two cold and damp little rooms behind the monastery, but they were among the best in the compound. Throughout the remainder of his life he would enjoy his visits there, but as he grew older, he found great hardship in the freezing winter fogs which plunged down from unknown heights, like an evanescent, icy waterfall.

9   The Old Bhutanese Palace

*Just as a white cloth will take any dye, so young children
are amenable to whatever training is given them. If the
training is of the right type, they will become good; if
otherwise, bad.*   (Dhardo Rimpoche)

During the summers of 1952 and 1953, Dhardo Rimpoche
spent long evenings in Kalimpong discussing events in
Tibet with other lamas and Tibetan nobles. They felt they
were watching, in appalled suspension, a chain of events
whose disastrous consequences they could forsee but
which they were powerless to avert. Rimpoche would say
'We must do something!' but they were not politicians,
and he was a Buddhist monk; there seemed to be nothing
they could do.

Rimpoche spent many nights turning these problems
over in his mind. As he did so, he gradually found that he
was turning for inspiration to the life of the previous
Dhardo Tulku. He recalled that, at their last meeting, the
thirteenth Dalai Lama had lavished praise on the previous
Dhardo Tulku, and had urged Rimpoche to follow his
example. He too had been a Buddhist monk, but he had
played a decisive role at the time of the earlier invasions.
It seemed to Rimpoche that his predecessor's principal
concern had been to preserve Tibetan culture as a means
of ensuring the survival of Buddhism. To do this, one did
not need to be a politician.

It was clear to those in Kalimpong that the refugees
already in the town would soon be joined by many others.
Already there were a number of Tibetan children in the
streets from poor families; there were even some orphans
struggling to find a way of living. Rimpoche and the

85

nobles knew for themselves how different life could be outside Tibet. They saw that children who grew up in India might have little sense of the culture that their parents had left behind.

What was needed, therefore, was a school which would ensure that the physical needs of children were met, but which would also offer them a traditional Tibetan education. A society was accordingly established to collect funds for such a school. But as the talk and the visions turned into work, most of the others dropped out, leaving Dhardo Rimpoche and Lobsang Lhalungpa to put the plans into effect.

Lhalungpa soon proved his worth by extracting funds from all kinds of sources. Whilst he gathered many donations from wealthy local Tibetans, he found that the greatest generosity came from the merchants who travelled to Kalimpong from Lhasa. These men were to be the mainstay of the school until Tibet was closed in 1959, when they could trade no more. The Dalai Lama was asked to lend the scheme his blessing and to give it financial support. 20,000 rupees were given for books, 15,000 for the library, 5,000 to run the society, and 10,000 for the land on which the school would stand. Rimpoche sold such effects as were not necessary to his household and contributed 4,000 rupees himself.

Government funding was found to be conditional upon the adoption of the approved Indian syllabus. This would mean that, in any one day, only forty-five minutes could be allotted to Tibetan subjects. But Rimpoche, in beginning to clarify his vision of the school as a guardian of Tibetan culture, saw that these conditions were unacceptable. They would go it alone.

In 1953, Rani Chunni Dorje granted Rimpoche the use of the old Bhutanese Palace as a home for the school. This was a large but ramshackle wooden building which had long since started to decay without quite losing a kind of shabby grandeur. At one time it had been the residence of the Bhutanese Government Agent. During his exile, in 1910, it had housed the thirteenth Dalai Lama. In accordance with custom, the room where the 'The Inmost One' had slept was left untouched after his departure, and was regarded as a shrine.

The benefactor, Rani Dorje, was the sister of the Maharaja of Sikkim. Although the Sikkimese royal family was by no means wealthy, the Rani had improved her lot by marrying a man below her station, S.T. Dorje. He was a man of humble origins who had made his fortune in business and had risen to become, effectively, the Chief Minister of Bhutan, and had been styled 'Raja' by the British. Although the leading member of the Buddhist community in Kalimpong, she was notoriously mean. Her gift of the use of the Palace was greeted with astonishment in the community, and it was sometimes said that she was secretly hoping that Rimpoche would effect some overdue repairs.

Undaunted by the rotten beams and leaking roof, and delighted by the size of the building, Rimpoche moved in and set about turning the ground floor into a school. On 10 December 1954, amidst much ceremony and celebration, the Indo-Tibetan Buddhist Cultural Institute School was opened. This was an important landmark in Rimpoche's life and a significant event in the struggle for the survival of Tibetan Buddhism. Though the beginnings were small the returns were great: it was now possible to receive a good traditional Tibetan education in India and, over time, a set of educated young men would appear in the Tibetan community who could speak English, Hindi, and Tibetan, and who were to prove invaluable.

In 1953, Rimpoche had been requested to contribute a section on Tibetan Buddhism to a book entitled *The Word of the Buddha*, by Kenneth Morgan. Since Rimpoche's English was not up to the task he offered to give the material to his helper Lobsang Lhalungpa. But Lhalungpa's written English was, at best, rudimentary. The more he worked on the text the more entangled it became, until the manuscript was in a dreadful state. He therefore took his work to the young man known to the Tibetans as Imji Gelong, 'English *bhikkhu*', and otherwise known as Sangharakshita. Sangharakshita found the manuscript somewhat badly written and confusing. He rewrote large sections, but, more often than not, sent Lhalungpa back to Rimpoche for clarification. This process was repeated several times until Sangharakshita had all but rewritten the text. In this way, through Lhalungpa, Sangharakshita came to learn much about Dhardo Tulku and was impressed by both his knowledge and his understanding of the Dharma. It was only a matter of time before Lhalungpa arranged a meeting. Both men had been living in Kalimpong for almost four years, and each knew the other by reputation, but Rimpoche had little idea that the Imji Gelong was the same Western *bhikkhu* whom he had seen from his window in Bodh Gaya.

At the age of sixteen, Sangharakshita had read two great classical Buddhist sutras and had experienced so powerful an insight into their meaning that he became a firm Buddhist. He travelled to India and, in 1949, at the age of twenty-four, was ordained as a Theravada *bhikkhu*. He became a pupil of the great scholar and revivalist monk, Jagdish Kashyap, who later instructed him to stay in Kalimpong 'and work for the good of the Dharma'. Here, among other things, he had founded the Young Men's Buddhist Association and a Buddhist journal called *Stepping Stones*.

In later life so many subsequent impressions intervened that neither man could remember much about their first meeting. At that time Sangharakshita was twenty-eight years old; he was tall and thin, he wore horn-rimmed spectacles over a prominent nose, and he dressed in the thin, ochre-coloured cotton robes of a Theravadin *bhikkhu*. His background was so different from that of a Tibetan that Rimpoche privately doubted whether the Imji Gelong could understand the Dharma in its depths or that he could follow the difficult life of a Buddhist monk. But when they started to discuss the Dharma, Rimpoche had the strong impression that Sangharakshita immediately grasped whatever he said, and that his understanding went far beyond mere book-learning.

From time to time Rimpoche had been considering going to the West to try to teach the Dharma there, but, following his contact with Sangharakshita, he changed his mind. Firstly, he realized that his own effectiveness would be limited by the language barrier. He had picked up rudimentary Hindi while working with the labourers at Bodh Gaya, and he had begun to recognize a few words of English through Nebesky-Wojkowitz's tuition, but he was clearly not a natural linguist. It became apparent to Rimpoche that the effort involved in mastering English would be better spent elsewhere. Secondly, he saw that his Buddhism was deeply embedded in Tibetan culture— which was very different to that of the West. Finally, he saw that he had, in Sangharakshita, a student who would be able to effect a translation of the Dharma into the terms of Western culture in his stead. Although it was to be another three years before the two men would come to know each another properly, their friendship was already important to both.

10 Buddha Jayanti

O Tree of Wisdom, Tree of Knowledge unsearchable,
Tree whereunder the world's deliverance was
  attained—
Through all the rain of years between our sight and thee,
Shall we not look back and behold and veil our faces?
For beneath this Tree was Wisdom perfected.[1]

Dhardo Rimpoche's monastery at Bodh Gaya overlooked
the spot where the Buddha gained Enlightenment. 1956–7
marked the passage of two-and-a-half millennia after the
Parinirvana, or death of the Buddha. This was Buddha
Jayanti year, and the Buddhist world celebrated vigorous-
ly. High Priests, Venerables, Eminences, and Holinesses
were called upon to give speeches in praise of the Buddha;
a great Council met whose delegates engaged in abstruse
debate about the text of the scriptures (and said hardly a
word about their spirit); and collections of articles
appeared in unprecedented numbers, discussing every
conceivable aspect of the Dharma. The sun of Buddhism,
which first rose at Bodh Gaya, had long since set in India,
but the Indians knew how brightly it continued to shine
in other skies, and wished to join the celebrations. The
Dalai Lama and a number of Buddhist royal families were
invited to visit India to offer incense at the holy places.
Dhardo Rimpoche invited the Dalai Lama to give a series
of public teachings at Bodh Gaya.

The visit was a great honour for Rimpoche, marking the
end of his isolation from the mainstream of the Tibetan
hierarchy. But this was to bring difficulties of its own.

[1] L. Adams Beck, *The Life of the Buddha*, Collins, 1959

Thousands came to listen to the Dalai Lama's words and to receive his blessing; more still were simply curious to see the young 'God-King of Tibet', about whom they had read in the newspapers. The Dalai Lama was now treated by the Chinese Communists as a subject of the People's Republic of China, and was kept under close surveillance throughout his visit. Nonetheless, he brought a full entourage. Meanwhile, the Panchen Lama, who traditionally had his own court a hundred miles from Lhasa, had also come to Bodh Gaya, and he too was closely guarded. He ranked second only to the Dalai Lama and, over the centuries, a degree of rivalry had grown up between the two courts. This was something that the Chinese had sought to exacerbate and exploit. There was potential for a security nightmare of politics and protocol.

On one occasion, the Dalai Lama's supporters thought that the Panchen Lama's throne was insultingly equal in height to the Dalai Lama's, so they tore it down and rebuilt it lower. Geshe Jampel Thardo remembered that 'some people thought Rimpoche was showing more respect to His Holiness the Dalai Lama than to His Eminence the Panchen Lama. Some of these people were partisans of the Panchen Lama and they became jealous.'

Rimpoche was devoted to both men as the spiritual heads of Tibetan Buddhism and this gossip caused him much pain, even though the Dalai Lama and Panchen Lama were both pleased with his arrangements. Later, the Dalai Lama travelled to Kalimpong—against the express wishes of the Chinese. He visited the ITBCI School, which delighted him, but was shocked to see the refugees and orphans who wandered the streets. This was a testament to the activities of the Chinese which the Dalai Lama suspected, but which had hitherto been hidden from him.

The importance of Bodh Gaya was growing in the minds of many Buddhists and this too brought problems.

Rimpoche was the abbot of the *gompa*, but he was also an official of the Tibetan government; he had jurisdiction over the monks, but there were also many Tibetan pilgrims; neither was his the only monastery nor the Tibetans the only visitors. In this rather confused situation an incident occurred, not long after the Dalai Lama's visit, which was to herald the beginning of a troubled relationship between Rimpoche and Tibetan officialdom.[1]

There was a tradition among Tibetan pilgrims, dating back longer than anyone could remember, of lighting butter-lamps beneath the Bodhi tree. The Maha Bodhi Temple had been forced by an Act of the Bihar State Government at Patna to hand over its affairs to a new management committee which included Buddhists. Anagarika Munindra Barua, the new manager of the temple, took exception to the Tibetan butter lamps. One day, Barua approached Rimpoche complaining, 'The Holy Tree will dry up and wither,' and demanded that he put an end to the practice. Rimpoche replied that butter-lamps had been burned long before his time and that the tree had shown no signs of decay. Barua still insisted, and Rimpoche explained that he had no authority over the Tibetan pilgrims and could not force them to refrain; the best solution would be to build a special platform, facing the tree, but situated a little distance away from it. He drew up a plan and told Barua that if he presented it to the local government at Patna they would probably provide the money. But Barua continued to complain, and a little later he approached a Tibetan Government official who was making a pilgrimage: 'Dhardo Rimpoche is killing the

[1] Dhardo Rimpoche had wished at the time to write something about the following events to clarify his position to the Tibetan Government, but had decided to let the matter rest. In interview with Dharmachari Kulamitra in November 1989 he said he was glad that, through this biography, the matter could be set straight.

Bodhi tree!' he exclaimed. The officer promptly stormed over to the Tibetan temple and began to abuse Rimpoche.

'Please don't speak like this,' Rimpoche replied, 'You are an important officer, but I am also appointed by your government. You must not speak in such a way. This tradition [of burning butter-lamps] reaches back to a time long before I came here. I have no power to stop it.'

'If you really cared about the Bodhi tree and the sacred place', replied the officer, 'you would do something about all the broken *stupas* and statues lying there.' But the remains lay in the grounds of the Maha Bodhi Temple and, as Rimpoche tried to explain, he had no authority to clear them up.

By this time a crowd had gathered, including many of the new monks at Rimpoche's *gompa* who had been attracted to stay after the Dalai Lama's visit. They were enraged by the officer's hostility to their abbot and by his foul language. Pilgrims gathered in increasing numbers and one monk, quite beside himself with indignation, slapped the official over the head. Other monks started to give him a sound thrashing. Barua shot off to the police station and returned with several police officers. By now, the crowd was enraged. The temple store-keeper let fly a stone, others followed, and a policeman was hurt. Eventually things calmed down and the crowd dispersed, but Barua took the Tibetan officer to the police station at Gaya and lodged a complaint. That evening they arrived at the *gompa* accompanied by policemen and the District Collector. He was a powerful local official, and an ex-officio chairman of the Temple Management Committee, with whom Rimpoche was on good terms.

'Today I've had very regrettable news,' he said.

'Yes', Rimpoche replied, 'It is most regrettable to me too. Two months ago I gave Barua a plan of what was required by the Tibetan pilgrims and asked him to approach the state government, but instead he has consistently provoked the pilgrims.'

Rimpoche denied inciting his monks to riot or to attack the Tibetan Officer. They had been provoked and had sought to defend their abbot.

'Just suppose,' he said to the Collector, 'an officer comes from another district and orders you to do something. Will you do it? I am in charge of this monastery, and I was appointed by the Tibetan Government. Of course this man is also a Tibetan officer but he is here on a pilgrimage—not to give orders.'

The District Collector took Rimpoche aside and whispered: 'Frankly this officer is a crank. Just forget about the whole thing.'

But he was unable to prevent the conviction of the temple store-keeper, and Rimpoche had to fight to get him freed. Whilst Barua and the official had acted unreasonably, and whilst Rimpoche had not been in the wrong, the actions of his followers had not been correct. A few months later there was still no offering platform, and Barua continued to complain. The Tibetan officer thought he had been badly treated and almost certainly influenced other Tibetan officials against Rimpoche.

As part of the Buddha Jayanti celebrations the Indian Government organized a tour of fifty-seven 'Eminent Buddhists from the Border Regions' to central India. They were taken to see Buddhist holy places, *stupas*, temples, and monasteries, and there were also visits to museums, factories, and government buildings. Rimpoche and Sangharakshita were chosen from Kalimpong whilst others came from Tibet, Sikkim, Bhutan, Kashmir, Ladakh, Assam, and other regions of the Himalayas. There were laymen and monks from the Tibetan traditions, but most conspicuous were the saffron-robed Theravadin monks who made a great point of observing the monastic obligations with even greater strictness than usual. No matter what, everything stopped when the time came for the Theravada *bhikkhus* to eat their meal, as stipulated, before noon. On the coaches, they would not sit with a layperson (as that would entail sitting on seats of equal height), and some insisted that Theravada *bhikkhus* should sit in the front of the coach, as this was considered the most prestigious position. Some of them refused even to acknowledge that Rimpoche and the other Tibetans were Buddhists at all.

Rimpoche's dealings with Theravada *bhikkhus* had been limited, and it must have seemed that the caricature of selfishness and individualism found in his own ancient canonical texts was being unwittingly re-enacted. Sangharakshita was used to this sort of thing and had come to expect an excess of formalism among the Theravadins; yellow robes notwithstanding, he sat at the back of the coach with Rimpoche. This was considered very bad form.

But these signs of spiritual moribundity were matched by unexpected signs of renewal. As the delegation passed through the slums on the outskirts of Agra, Sangharakshita spotted a sign showing directions to a Buddhist temple. When he enquired, the officials denied that any such temple existed, but Sangharakshita had seen the notice and, since there was time, he insisted that they should visit it. None of the other eminent Buddhists showed the slightest interest in the venture, so Sangharakshita announced that he, at the very least, would go. Rimpoche, impressed by his persistence, agreed to accompany him.

Together they hired a motor rickshaw and, after considerable difficulty, located the temple. There was no one around, so Sangharakshita rang the temple bell. Eventually, local people arrived and stared in bewilderment at the two red- and yellow-robed monks. These people were former Hindu 'Untouchables' who had recently embraced Buddhism in the wave of mass-conversions started by their leader, Dr Ambedkar. Now, only weeks later, two monks had come all the way to their temple; a Hindu 'holy man' would never have visited them. They were not sure of the proper way to welcome a Buddhist monk, but they showed great courtesy and hospitality. Rimpoche's Hindi was poorer than that of Sangharakshita, so he was content mainly to listen as Sangharakshita talked to them. He was moved by Sangharakshita's great kindness and warmth and by the encouragement he showed the 'New Buddhists' to persevere on their chosen path. Few Buddhists of the Himalayan regions had heard of this wave of conversions among the Untouchables, and Rimpoche was keen to discover how these people, the very poorest and least regarded in India, had deserted Hinduism to become Buddhists.

The party arrived at Delhi where they were to meet the Indian President, Rajendra Prasad. There being some time beforehand, Sangharakshita organized a meeting with Dr Ambedkar himself. Ambedkar had been born an Untouchable, but had risen to become India's first Law Minister and the architect of her constitution. His stature was such that he could speak for the hundreds of millions of Untouchables across India, but, even as a member of the government, he had been able to obtain few concessions for them. In disgust, he turned from politics to religion. After years of careful consideration, he had chosen Buddha Jayanti year to renounce Hinduism within which, he understood, his people would always be seen in terms of caste, and pledged his life to the path of Buddhism. At a historic meeting, he performed the ceremony in which several hundreds of thousands of his followers also converted. A wave of mass conversions had started and, within weeks, there were said to be several million 'New'

Buddhists. Every day the numbers were swelling as community after community renounced 'the hell of caste' for the purity of Buddhism.

Sangharakshita had come to know Ambedkar as a result of some correspondence and two meetings, but this was the first time they had met since the conversions. There was cause for celebration, but also for great anxiety. Sangharakshita records that he led Rimpoche and 'some two or three dozen colourfully clad monks, nuns, and laymen' to Ambedkar's house in Delhi.

> 'The Eminent Buddhists from the Border Regions sat facing Ambedkar in a semi-circle, with the sunlight falling on the vivid magentas, oranges, and yellows of their robes. Ambedkar himself sat behind a small table, Mrs Ambedkar beside him. He wore a light tropical suit and a pith helmet, and looked so old and so ill that I felt obliged to apologize for our troubling him'.[1]

Dhardo Rimpoche and the others watched as Ambedkar talked to Sangharakshita 'in so low a voice' that he had to go 'quite close in order to catch what he was saying.' Rimpoche looked on in amazement as the worn out figure seemed to weaken by the minute.

> 'His head gradually sank until it almost touched his outstretched arms, which were resting on the surface of the table. Sitting there in that way, like an Atlas for whom the globe had at last become too heavy for him to bear, he spoke about his hopes and fears—mostly fears—for the movement of conversion to Buddhism he had inaugurated.... There was still so much to be done, the sad, tired voice was saying ... so much to

[1] from *Ambedkar and Buddhism*

be done.... Eventually the great leader's eyes closed in sheer weariness'.

Dhardo Rimpoche had expected an entirely different sort of figure from Sangharakshita's descriptions—tall, strong, robust. What he saw instead was a man with a weary and broken frame, but he realized that it contained the heart of a great man, perhaps a Bodhisattva, like the great Tibetan religious kings who lived a thousand years ago. Even they had only created the conditions for conversions, while Ambedkar had been directly responsible for leading millions of men and women to embrace the Dharma.

Such incidents afforded fascinating glimpses of worlds that were quite new to Dhardo Rimpoche. For his part, he could easily have gained a reputation among the delegates as a kind of benign oracle. On one occasion, the party was told that they were to visit a dam, only to find themselves arriving at a Buddhist temple with not a stick of incense between them. But Rimpoche opened his voluminous robe and took from the folds of his cloak enough offering incense and packets of candles for everyone. Later, when the delegates were meeting the Vice-President, Radhakrishnan, they were again surprised to be suddenly introduced to Jawarhalal Nehru, the Prime Minister. But Dhardo Rimpoche took from his robe a beautiful Tibetan scroll painting, mounted in precious silks, and presented it to the Prime Minister along with an offering scarf and his name-card. Before leaving Kalimpong he had ordered the painting for exactly this eventuality. Sangharakshita, meanwhile, performed some still more efficacious magic at the reception with the President. He had been delegated to deliver a speech thanking the Indian Government for its hospitality. Having discussed with Rimpoche the problems he was having at Bodh Gaya, Sangharakshita mentioned them in the course of his speech. The President took the point and the platform which Rimpoche had designed so many months before was erected soon after.

This was the first time that Rimpoche had been without his attendants or one of his relations, but he said that travelling with Sangharakshita was like travelling with family. They found delight and stimulation in each other's company and began to realize that they were of one mind.

11 The Demon of Eclipse

They blame the man who is silent,
They blame the man who speaks too much,
And they blame the man who speaks too little.
No man can escape blame in this world.[1]

Tibet was conquered by degrees. For a while Tibetans continued to order the civil administration while Chinese troops infested Lhasa, but the phantom of Tibetan authority was gradually overwhelmed by the demon of Chinese power. Day by day, as Chinese demands grew more outrageous, their tone became more insistent. An official attempting to infiltrate Tibetan values into his work would end up trying to save his own head. In Lhasa there were daily reports of arrests, torture, and summary execution. In the provinces, petty merchants, peasants, and nomads found that their merchandise, livestock, and land had been confiscated. To object could mean death.

In the seclusion of the Summer Palace, the Dalai Lama was out of the hands of the Chinese and out of sight of their actions. But he symbolized the vestige of autonomy to which the Tibetans clung so tenaciously. Then, in March 1959, the Chinese issued him with an invitation to a celebration in their military camp; it seemed difficult to refuse and dangerous to accept. His concern was to placate the Chinese in order to prevent them from massacring his people, but the Tibetan people preferred to risk their own lives rather than see the Dalai Lama placed in danger. Thirty thousand Tibetans surrounded the Summer Palace to prevent him from leaving and the Chinese from

[1] *The Dhammapada*, trans. Juan Mascaro, Penguin, 1973

entering. Inside, the Dalai Lama spent agonising days afraid of the threat from which he was being guarded—and fearing for the safety of his guards. Outside, the demands of the crowd grew more strident, and the protest threatened to turn into a full-scale revolt. One night, as the tension mounted, and as the Chinese ordered an end to the protests, the Dalai Lama slipped out, along with his family, his attendants, and his tutors.

The entourage fled to India. Two days later, Chinese guns opened fire on the Palace, the Potala fortress, the Holy Jokang Temple, on the surrounding monasteries, and eventually on the whole city. Thousands were killed. Tibet had fallen, but the Dalai Lama was alive.

In Kalimpong, Rimpoche performed *pujas* both for the Dalai Lama's safety and for that of his people. Finally, the newspapers announced that the 'God-King' had arrived safely in India, and Rimpoche shed tears of relief. Then, over the snowy Himalayan passes, the refugees started to pour into the town. The first to arrive were monks whose monasteries had been shelled and whose teachers had been arrested. Then came peasants from the border regions. Finally, there came the scarred and traumatized survivors of the massacres in Lhasa and elsewhere. The eastern provinces were held most strongly by the Chinese, and escape was much more difficult. But the dangers involved in staying outweighed those of leaving, and refugees soon came from there, too, across unguarded but treacherous passes. Time and again, Rimpoche asked about relatives and friends. Sometimes there was no news, but at other times he would be told of people who had found their escape routes cut off and who were now in the hands of the Chinese. Some of his friends were imprisoned and tortured, and others were even executed. As people were shipped to labour camps, re-education schools, or factories across China, many families, including some that

Rimpoche had known, were divided, perhaps forever. Kalimpong and Darjeeling were in crisis. First there was poverty and then there was famine; monks were disrobing in order to work, and children were stealing in order to eat. The Indian government set up resettlement camps, but the refugees who left found themselves separated from their families on the burning Indian plains. Only too often they succumbed to the heat or contracted diseases against which they had no resistance. Peasants, merchants, monks, and nobles were, all alike, destitute. They lined the streets in Kalimpong, selling whatever they had brought with them: a turquoise earring, a butter-lamp, a wooden cup, or a fragment of a religious text. Rimpoche saw monks being taken away in lorry-loads to work on the roads throughout India. Even older monks struggled to learn a craft by which they might feed themselves.

Then there were the orphaned children. Some had tagged along behind refugees; there were others whose parents had perished in the bitter cold of the winter and the rigours of the trek. Rimpoche watched them as they thronged the streets and begged or stole for their food. He was already looking after some orphans, so it was natural for him to open an ITBCI orphanage. The Indian Government made a contribution to its upkeep but there was precious little money nevertheless. Soon the orphanage was full to the point of overflowing; it housed over fifty children and, everywhere Rimpoche went, there were more.

The leading Tibetans in Kalimpong now formed an association to address the problems of the refugees; it included several important *tulkus*, Tibetan Government officials, and a brother of the Dalai Lama. At first, Dhardo Rimpoche lent full support to this venture as a means of finding practical answers to pressing problems. But, as time passed, the issues with which the association was dealing impinged on the broader question of how the Tibetans would be governed outside Tibet. Some wanted the Government-in-exile to have complete authority over all Tibetans in India; in effect, they wanted to create a state within a state. These were the people who had ruled at home, and they now wished to maintain their authority even in the beleaguered circumstances to which they had been reduced. Although Dhardo Rimpoche had been born into the aristocracy, he was immune to the coaxing and cajoling of his peers. The association polarized into two camps, Rimpoche speaking out vehemently against the policies of members of the Government. In this way he held fast to the interests of the people, but he made many enemies.

Dhardo Rimpoche's concern to see a different kind of government was matched by his concern for continuity of religious practice. Monks from the great colleges had been resettled in several different areas, and their studies had effectively come to an end. There was particular concern about the closure of the Tantric colleges where the great cycles of Tantric texts and their rituals had been passed on. Although Rimpoche had only spent some eight or nine months at Gyu-Med, the colleges had a special place in his heart and he considered them essential to the survival of Tibetan Buddhism. He was deeply indebted to the great lamas who taught there, and could still be extremely apologetic for not having completed his Tantric studies— as if he did not regard himself as a fully qualified lama on that account.

The officers of the Government-in-exile had attempted to sort out these problems, but few of them were fluent in Hindi or English; fewer still were conversant with the mores of Indian politics or the circuitous workings of Indian officialdom. Rimpoche, by contrast, had been in India for ten years and had had many dealings with officials. His Hindi had improved and, although his grammar was erratic and his accent thick, he no longer had to work through a translator. There were also several students from the school who were now fluent in Tibetan, Hindi, and English. Rechung Tulku and a number of *geshes* who had settled in Kalimpong therefore pleaded with him to help re-establish the Tantric colleges. Others complained that the Tibetan officers had achieved nothing in the course of several months.

Rimpoche set off, with several *geshes* and some of the school's best students, to Gangtok, in Sikkim, where there was an Indian political officer with whom Rimpoche had very good relations. The officer immediately put a call through to the Government in Delhi. By that evening, monks from the Tantric colleges had been allocated 275 places in Dalhousie, a hill-station in Himachal Pradesh. Rimpoche moved to Dalhousie and worked with his team of helpers, tracking down the former lamas, Rimpoches, and students. Within a month, he had gathered the most important teachers who were living in India. He had achieved in a few weeks what the Tibetan officials had not been able to do in six months.

But he worried that this success would simply exacerbate the resentment of his enemies in the Government-in-exile. The officer who had taken a beating in Bodh Gaya some years previously was now actively maligning him, and he had powerful enemies among the most important officers in Kalimpong. The other lamas told him not to worry as the Dalai Lama would be very pleased with his work. Several of the college's top Rimpoches went to see the Dalai Lama and wrote back saying that this was, indeed, the case and that the Dalai Lama had requested Rimpoche to stay until the work was complete. Nonetheless, he decided to seek an audience of his own.

It was a long interview covering many topics, but

Rimpoche left feeling assured that the Dalai Lama appreciated his work and did not see it as an interference in government business. Outside the audience chamber, however, Rimpoche was faced by the Dalai Lama's subordinates. Over the centuries, the office of the Dalai Lama had grown increasingly political. Those who surrounded him were, first and foremost, politicians. Rimpoche found himself exposed to their rebukes and disdain.

He was deeply upset. He thought for days about the strength of the hostility which he seemed to have excited, and contemplated its possible consequences. He considered the directness and outspokenness of his character and concluded that it was inimical to dealing with those who held political power. He had already stirred up a hornet's nest and had exposed himself, his school, his orphanage, and his monasteries to the sting. Moreover, he was liable to be asked to do more such work. At last, he took a solemn oath: never again would he do anything which would involve him in government work. This oath marked a turning point in his life, and his worldly *importance* was henceforth to diminish—even if his outspokenness was not. On several occasions the Dalai Lama asked him to take up other offices. One was a position in Dharamsala dealing with cultural and religious affairs; another was a place as a representative of the Gelugpa school on a council representing all the Tibetan Buddhist schools. On one occasion he was requested to take over the administration of all Tibetan primary and secondary schools in India. Each time Rimpoche excused himself by citing his vow.

In spite of what had happened, Rimpoche's respect for the Dalai Lama was boundless. The thirteenth Dalai Lama had recognized him as a *tulku*, appointed his tutor, and performed his ordination as a novice monk. Rimpoche kept framed photographs of him high on the walls of his room, just below his photographs of the fourteenth Dalai Lama. For Rimpoche, the Dalai Lama was the principal lama of Tibetan Buddhism, an embodiment of the principle of compassion. It was therefore of crucial importance that the relationship be kept in good repair. But the Dalai Lama was very young, he was new to government, and he was not yet fully in control of his entourage. His officials would deny access to those who were out of favour with them and, after the interview in Dharamsala, Rimpoche was not able to contact the Dalai Lama in person or in writing for some years. To the Dalai Lama's great credit he eventually ceased letting himself be controlled in this way, and took a firmer hold on his entourage. But, in the meantime, the estrangement was a cause of great sadness to Rimpoche, and denied him a powerful friend.

Now that he was vulnerable, Rimpoche faced a wilderness of troubles. In later life, he rarely spoke about them, and hardly at all in the preparation of this biography. But while they need not be dwelt on at length, their seriousness should not be underestimated. Tibetan officials ordered Rimpoche to close the ITBCI School as the Tibetan Government-in-exile was to open an 'official' school in Kalimpong. Rimpoche held his ground. The Dalai Lama had given his blessing when the school was opened and he had not withdrawn it. Only if he did so would the school be closed. Such defiance increased Rimpoche's already substantial popularity with the Tibetan community, many of whose children were being educated at Rimpoche's personal expense. Rimpoche maintained control of his school and the purity of its syllabus. An 'official' school did open and, for a while, it grew much larger than the ITBCI School. But it achieved this by accepting government funding, and kept Tibetan subjects to a minimum.

At one point it seemed possible that Chinese policy towards Tibet had changed and that there was a chance that independence might be restored. The diplomats were greatly excited, but Rimpoche was sceptical. When people started returning to Tibet he spoke out against it in forcible terms—only to find that he had alienated the officers even further. There were accusations that he was no longer Tibetan, and had already surrendered to the Indian Government. At other times, perhaps because of his concern for the ordinary people, rumours were circulated that Rimpoche was in the employ of Chinese communists who were secretly funding his school. The Tibetan community did not believe this for a moment, but the truth can be corroded, and Rimpoche had to take great care in his dealings with Indian government officials. Later still, it was put about that he was in the employ of the Nationalist Chinese and that his support came from Formosa. Rimpoche had many friends in Kalimpong and was able to keep ahead of his opponents, but his difficulties were becoming very serious. According to one incarnate lama, it was popularly believed that there was, at one point, even a plot to do away with the 'meddlesome Rimpoche'. Whether or not this was the case, it shows how high feelings had run. Often Rimpoche would recount these difficulties to Sangharakshita, remarking, however, that the main thing which bothered him was that he no longer had access to the Dalai Lama. That was a spiritual relationship; the rest was just politics. When the man suspected of being at the head of the murder plot died, Rimpoche performed his funeral ceremonies without bearing the slightest grudge.

The troubles culminated in 1962, at the Bodh Gaya *gompa*. There were now between fifty and sixty monks, most of whom greatly appreciated Rimpoche, but a few still resented his strictness. The disaffected monks approached the lay and monastic officers appointed to the *gompa* by the Tibetan Government with their complaints.

The officers, who may have been influenced by Rimpoche's reputation, concluded that it would be better for all concerned if he were to step down. Rimpoche told them, 'You should look at the facts, starting from the time I came here. You should examine the work and the progress during my time as *khenpo*. You may also enquire from other people who know me here in the temple, and amongst people in Kalimpong.' But the officials would not listen; there was no one to whom he might have recourse, and Rimpoche had to leave.

The post of *khenpo* at Bodh Gaya lay vacant for several years until it was filled by the Dalai Lama's junior tutor. After his death, Tara Tulku became *khenpo*. He told me that, even today, the monastery is run according to the same programme, and by the same rules, that Dhardo Rimpoche had devised. Although Rimpoche had already achieved much in the *gompa*, he had had many plans for its further development. He was bitterly disappointed at losing this job, and it was hard not to see it as a personal indictment. The ITBCI School was working to preserve Tibetan culture among the young, but the monastery was giving a training in Buddhist study and ritual. For Rimpoche, the two went hand in hand. Returning to Kalimpong, he engaged in a study of the political and ecclesiastical history of Tibet. Here he found many cases similar to his own that had occurred down the centuries among kings, ministers, ambassadors, treasurers, merchants, and abbots. Institutions required leaders, and monasteries were no exception. But those who had to lead the institutions were always liable to attack.

In Kalimpong Rimpoche still had much to do. He was now able to devote his time more fully to the orphanage and the school, but harder blows were yet to fall. The *ITBCI Report 1954–1962* tells a brief and sad tale:

'For two years and five months, Dhardo Rimpoche was running a hostel in a rented building for Tibetan orphans, 52 of them in all, both boys and girls. All those who saw it praised it as a model of order and cleanliness.... Their upkeep was no light matter and the Rimpoche had a grant from the Government of India.... Even with this the Rimpoche found it hard to make ends meet but was forced to do so as no funds were available elsewhere. This government assistance continued up to the end of the last financial year (28 February 1962), since when nothing further has been received.

'This has had dire results for many children in the orphanage, which, being without money to continue, has had to close. The children so happily accommodated in it have either had to leave Kalimpong, or are being prematurely forced into work, or are merely idling on the streets.

'Out of the 52 in the orphanage, Rimpoche has managed to keep with him 29 who now have to sleep in the school premises.... Of those remaining, ten are small boys who somehow support themselves here and there (by collecting small amounts of food and money in Kalimpong). 13 older boys maintain themselves by making Tibetan felt boots, and 6 girls scrape along spinning woollen thread.'

The report warned that 'this has been a serious setback and has thrown many young boys onto the streets, into the arms of waiting missionaries'. In its boldest type, the report announced that there were a further 'two hundred orphans' in Kalimpong.

Then, without any warning, Rani Chunni Dorje suddenly announced that Rimpoche would have to leave the Bhutanese Palace, although she knew his predicament. He

109

could not understand the order, or the callous manner in which it was delivered. Rimpoche had recently performed the funeral rituals for the Rani's husband, and had created, he felt, a special link between himself and the Rani. Sangharakshita remarked that he had never seen Rimpoche so upset as at this time, not even with all his other troubles.

The school was close to disaster. Many parents could not afford to look after their children, and the ITBCI School was their only source of refuge. Without it many of the hundred or so pupils would, like the orphans, be thrust onto the streets or have to go out to work.

In 1963, darkness shrouded the future of the school and Rimpoche introduced the School Report with a plea for help:

'It has become necessary for the school to acquire premises of its own, together with a playground and industrial block, as well as to make arrangements for the maintenance of the poorer students. Thus there is a greater need for financial help than ever before. In the world of today people are exerting themselves in the cause of religion and culture and we see that on all sides support is being given to such exertions. The religion and culture of Buddhism are more in accordance with modern requirements than any others. Consequently one might expect that there should be a proportionately greater number of people ready to help us. In this confidence I am issuing the Report.'

These problems were part of a greater gloom which had enveloped the Tibetan people:

'Dark clouds have arisen from all quarters and the brilliance of the sun of religion and culture has been overcast. Especially from the east the demon of eclipse has, it seems, greedily devoured the sun.'

12 Shri Lama Rimpoche

O my own Immediate Shri Lama Rimpoche (abiding)
  within the lotus of my heart,
May you never separate from me but, on the contrary,
  remain inseparable!
Throughout all births may I have an excellent guru and,
From him never separated, may I practise the Shri
  Dharma[1]

Several years after the exodus, the position of most
Tibetans remained desperate. Some emigrated to the
United States, Britain, Canada, Switzerland, and elsewhere. Many of these people set up in business and some
prospered; in the 1970s, *tulkus* and *geshes* started to teach
Westerners who were interested in the Dharma. But many
Tibetans were still living in the refugee camps on the
plains, infested with malaria and tuberculosis. Slowly,
little colonies grew up around the camps where the
majority of the 100,000 Tibetans in India still live. The
largest monasteries were also able to reassemble themselves in miniature, but their circumstances could be appalling; Drepung was rehoused in a former British prison
and many of its one thousand inhabitants died before a
better location could be found. The crisis slowly receded,
although, right up to the present day, the monks are
uniformly poor and the laity poorer still. Over the years,
however, they have been able to build several beautiful
monasteries where the wheel of the Dharma continues to
turn.

[1] *The Easy Path to Emancipation*, trans. Sangharakshita and Dhardo
Rimpoche, published privately.

As the Tibetans dispersed across India, Kalimpong became a much quieter town. Deprived of its trade-links with Lhasa, it turned, gradually, into a rather secluded Himalayan backwater. As it did so, Rimpoche's difficulties with the Tibetan officials slowly diminished as they moved away or just chose to ignore him. The ITBCI School eventually found alternative accommodation and, a few years after their interview, the Dalai Lama visited Kalimpong in 1975, met Rimpoche, and made it clear to everyone that he was delighted with his work and with that of the school. Although the school was to experience repeated financial crises, it managed to survive, and Rimpoche's life assumed, more or less, the shape it retained until his death. He was the director of the ITBCI and the abbot of Yi Ga Choling Gompa. Above all, he explored the depths of meditation; he was a spiritual friend, and he was a teacher.

The Buddhist life of the Himalayas is many centuries old and characterized by the giving and receiving of initiations. A lama sits high up on a throne, dressed in full monastic regalia, and expounds a teaching, a ritual, or a meditation practice which he has himself received from one of his teachers. In this manner, Rimpoche happily gave the more general initiations which demanded only a moderate commitment. He taught long-life and protection initiations, simple meditations on the most popular Bodhisattvas, like Tara or Avalokiteshvara; he performed rituals for the benefit of the community and in celebration of special festivals. In this way Rimpoche had a role as teacher to the Buddhist community, which allowed him to display one of his most distinctive gifts: the ability to communicate his understanding to ordinary people. He would listen to anyone who came to him, and if he could offer advice, he would do so; if only words of encouragement were needed, he would find them. This ability to make a connection with ordinary experience helped make him a popular public speaker. When Sangharakshita organized programmes of speakers he found that most lamas had to be briefed in advance about their delivery, but Rimpoche could speak clearly and fluently. His words were bold, outspoken, and honest.

However, it was known that the lamas who had fled to the Himalayan foothills had brought with them hitherto inaccessible teachings and rituals; for the first time in five centuries, practitioners of the prized and secret 'Tantric Path' were to be found in India. The lamas felt that the spiritually immature would have only a vulgar and literal understanding of its symbols, and were wary of mis-interpretation and abuse. They rarely communicated any-thing of the Tantra to individuals who did not practise and appreciate traditional Buddhism. Rimpoche gave higher initiations only to monks who specifically required them, or to laymen who were capable of keeping the formidable commitments involved. Numerous Western scholars sought Rimpoche's advice and, generally, he was accom-modating. But the sexual imagery and awesome practices of the Tantra had, naturally, exerted their own particular fascination.

On one occasion, Prince Peter of Greece and Denmark, a well known Tibetologist, visited Rimpoche with a Western scholar who had only a limited grasp of the Dharma. The scholar proceeded, nonetheless, to inter-rogate Rimpoche about Tantra. Resorting to the polite Tibetan custom of quoting proverbs, Rimpoche replied with the Tibetan equivalent of 'one should not cast pearls before swine.' Prince Peter turned to the scholar and remarked in English, 'He probably doesn't know anything about the Tantra anyway.' Knowing at least enough English to understand what the prince had said Rimpoche could hardly contain his mirth as he afterwards related the episode to Sangharakshita.

Sangharakshita, at any rate, observed that there was something rather remarkable about Dhardo Rimpoche. On one occasion, the house of one of his Nepali friends had been mysteriously plagued by stones the size of a fist, which had been crashing onto the roof. Many people had seen the stones apparently fall from the sky, but the strangest thing was that each stone was marked by the Arabic numeral '4' or a cross. The family was understandably terrified, as a blow from a single stone could be fatal. Sangharakshita approached Rimpoche for help, and he thought the matter over and said he was convinced that the house was the target of black magic; someone bore the family intense hatred and wished to kill them. Shortly after his visit, the stoning stopped. When Sangharakshita asked what he had done, Rimpoche replied, with a wry smile and a twinkle in his eye: 'A bit of *puja!*'

Sangharakshita now had his own vihara, or monastery, in Kalimpong, a couple of miles from the ITBCI School, and found himself working a good deal with Dhardo Rimpoche. Lobsang Phuntsok Lhalungpa had disrobed and married, taking up the post of head of the Tibetan Section of All-India Radio in Delhi. He was occasionally able to help in raising funds for the school, but Rimpoche was now without a translator or secretary. Sangharakshita was happy to help him with his correspondence, and Rimpoche often made the walk from the school to the vihara. Although he knew Sangharakshita was a writer, he always, but always, arrived carrying his own typing-paper and carbon. They often discussed their latest thoughts, and Sangharakshita found himself increasingly impressed by Rimpoche's knowledge and understanding of Buddhism. At that time, virtually no Tibetan texts had been translated into English. It was clear that he was extremely fortunate to have met and become the friend of a lama of Dhardo Rimpoche's calibre.

The Dalai Lama has commented, rather wryly, that 'the Chinese did the Tibetans a favour by forcing them to purify their religion, which had become obsessed with form and splendour at the expense of content.'[1] Geshe Lhundup had insisted that Rimpoche should always dwell on the content of what he studied and, in the years that followed, he had diligently and methodically attempted to put this into practice. He had carefully examined hundreds of Dharma texts, consulted their commentaries, reflected on their context, and meditated upon their meaning. As a result, Dhardo Rimpoche was able to open for Sangharakshita the treasure-house of the Tibetan canon, and show him its precious contents.

The teacher found that he could also learn from his pupil. Before meeting Sangharakshita, Dhardo Rimpoche had been accustomed to teaching in the 'classical' style, seated on a throne while his disciples sat below. Traditionally, the lama is regarded, at such times, as the very Buddha himself and it must be difficult to feel anything for him other than profound awe. While teacher-disciple bonds were usually very strong, Rimpoche commented that it was rare for a lama to develop a close *friendship* with a pupil. Thus it came as a revelation when he realized that something remarkable had developed between himself and Sangharakshita. They had become intimate friends.

The two monks had come together through personal contact rather than through any formal connection; theirs was indeed a triumph of friendship over the divisions of culture, nationality, and sect. They had met as fellow Buddhists who discovered that they shared a commitment to understanding the truth and to practising their religion, rather than to performing the duties of a particular

[1] from *Great Ocean*

tradition. Sangharakshita was always disgusted with the
'canker of formalism'[1] and had been frustrated by its
prominence in the Theravada, the school into which he
had been ordained. As he had come into contact with a
variety of Buddhist schools he was increasingly concerned
to understand what constituted the 'unifying factor' of
Buddhism. In time, he identified this as the shared commitment to Buddhist ideals, or 'Going for Refuge', which
had linked him with Dhardo Rimpoche.

However, at the time of writing *A Survey of Buddhism*,
between 1954 and 1956, he had found this unifying factor
in the Bodhisattva who is the embodiment of these ideals.
This figure was 'the perfectly ripened fruit of the whole
tree of Buddhism' (p.391). He had responded 'like a gong
that has been struck' to 'the ideal of dedicating oneself, for
innumerable life-times, to the attainment of Supreme Enlightenment for the benefit of all living beings.'[2] Such was
the impact that Sangharakshita felt impelled to seek Bodhisattva ordination in order to give 'formal expression' to
his response.

But the Bodhisattva is not an 'airy' ideal. It may take up,
in a human being, 'a local habitation and a name'. Thus,
while Sangharakshita never regarded Dhardo Rimpoche
as a living Buddha, he did regard him as an exemplar of
Buddhist ideals. He observed in Rimpoche a generous and
caring spirit and a remarkable degree of selflessness.
When Sangharakshita came to recount the 'History of My
Going For Refuge' he recalled that, at last, 'I had found a
preceptor from whom I could take the ordination. This
was Dhardo Rimpoche ... whom I had come to revere as
being himself a living Bodhisattva.'

For Sangharakshita, therefore, the friendship offered a

[1] *A Survey of Buddhism* 6th ed. p.xv
[2] *The History of My Going For Refuge*, p.71

context in which he could train in the path which led to the heart of Buddhism with a man who seemed to dwell within it. 'Dhardo Rimpoche ... not only gave me the Bodhisattva ordination but subsequently explained the sixty-four Bodhisattva precepts to me in considerable detail.' And the teacher seems to have been content with the progress of his pupil. Rimpoche recalled:

'When we talked about profound aspects of Buddhism he had no difficulty at all in understanding them—with ease. Not only this but, at the same time, he was able to put it all into practice and teach others. Ordinary people cannot understand deep points of Dharma so easily and are not in a position to teach to others. His high level of motivation and dedication to the study of Buddhism encouraged and inspired me to study Buddhism even more seriously and in greater depth.'

Not only did Rimpoche embody for Sangharakshita the fruit of Buddhist ideals, but he encouraged him to become acquainted with the varieties of its flowers. By good fortune Sangharakshita picked up a Nyingmapa text called 'The Easy Path to Emancipation' in the Kalimpong bazaar. Kachu Rimpoche, one of his Nyingmapa teachers, had recently granted him permission to practise the meditations, but the text was in Tibetan. Rimpoche was delighted to help by providing a translation in broken Hindi which Sangharakshita, in turn, translated into English. By this procedure they produced a remarkably accurate and poetic translation which Sangharakshita was to use for several years. Rimpoche said:

'I told Sangharakshita that there is no basic difference between the various sects of Tibetan Buddhism— Gelugpa, Nyingmapa, Kagyupa, and Shakyapa—it's just a matter of approach and style which individual

lamas have influenced. Otherwise, the source is one;
it is the Buddha. The different schools are all part of
the Mahayana Buddhist tradition.'

Sangharakshita's own monastery, the Triyana Vardhana
Vihara, was dedicated to the development of the non-
sectarian approach to Buddhism which Dhardo Rimpoche
so warmly encouraged. In 1961 Rimpoche attended a spectacular demonstration of these principles in a festival dedicated to Tsongkhapa, the founder of his own Gelugpa
school. It was organized by Sangharakshita under the
auspices of the vihara and the Kalimpong branch of the
Maha Bodhi Society.

'Proceedings began ... with a colourful procession
more than half a mile long. First came a contingent of
Tibetan monks, in ceremonial dress of gorgeous silk
brocade, some carrying banners of victory, others
playing drums, trumpets, and conch-shells. Lastly,
borne in a golden palanquin under a huge umbrella
of yellow silk, came a famous gold image of
Tsongkapa.'[1]

High ranking lamas from almost every Tibetan tradition
attended. Later, Rimpoche said that he had never heard of
such a meeting of the 'rival' schools, even in Tibet.

In 1963, Sangharakshita helped to prepare the 1963
ITBCI School Report, and translated Rimpoche's introduc-
tion into English. In this, Rimpoche wrote in a tone of
considerable urgency: 'One acre of land near the bazaar is
available, the price being Rs 12,000. We appeal to all our
friends and well-wishers to help us in raising this amount
before the end of the year.'

As a result of these appeals, many people, even the
poorest, came forward with funds. Sangharakshita helped

[1] *Maha Bodhi Journal,* January, 1961

to write letters to people and organizations in London, outlining the situation and appealing for funds. The 1963 *Report* gratefully acknowledges donations from 'The Tibet Society, London, the Canadian Tibetan Refugee Society, the Elmshurst Trust, UK, Christmas Humphreys, and students of Holy Cross County Primary School, UK (this last raised by carol-singing, sale of Christmas cards, and Sunday school collection).' The piece of land was soon purchased, and the two-storeyed wooden structures, which I saw when I first visited the school, were built.

Not long after this, in 1964, Sangharakshita received a letter from the English Sangha Trust in London. There had been a split in the Buddhist community in England, and it was hoped that, as the seniormost British Buddhist monk, he might be able to reconcile the two sides. At first he was not inclined to take up the invitation; he already had commitments to his literary work, to the ex-Untouchable Buddhists, and to activities in Kalimpong and Darjeeling. But he discussed the invitation with others who knew the situation, and consulted his teachers. Rimpoche felt that it was his duty to go and that it might be a fine opportunity to spread the Dharma in the West; Sangharakshita accepted the invitation and decided to leave India late in the summer of 1964.

Rimpoche returned to the work of developing the school. He was assisted by several teachers who had been with him since the inauguration of the school, such as Tashi Dorje, the dance-master. But, in the two years that Sangharakshita was away, he had the particular help of two young Tibetans who were later to provide him with great support. The first was a young *tulku*, called Ventul (or Bentul) Rimpoche, who had been entrusted to his care by Drepung's Loseling College. The second was Jampel Kaldhen, whom Rimpoche had sent for from Tibet, along with his brother, in 1956. Both helped by teaching in the school, and Jampel prepared Tibetan grammar books. He was the grandson of the previous Dhardo Tulku's steward. In due course he became Rimpoche's steward and, eventually, took over the day-to-day running of the school.

Although Rimpoche had grown isolated from the Tibetan hierarchy, he had many friends in Kalimpong. Tri-Ngawang Rimpoche was a *tulku* of a previous Ganden Tripa who had been a friend of the previous Dhardo Rimpoche. In this life he had studied at Drepung, where he had been a few years junior to Rimpoche; but they had often debated together, and had become close friends. The Chinese had sent Tri-Ngawang Rimpoche to a labour camp for several years, but he had been a model inmate and the guards had become lax. Eventually, he saw an opportunity to escape with a fellow prisoner, Nechung Rimpoche, but, to make the escape really worthwhile, they decided to take something of great value out of Tibet.

Nechung Rimpoche had been the abbot of a monastery where one of the state oracle-priests had once had his seat. The monastery housed a container in which, it was believed, there resided the soul of the oracle who spoke through the priest. They determined to rescue this receptacle from where it had been carefully hidden. However, when they retrieved it, it was so heavy that they despaired of being able to carry it across the mountains. But as the lamas fled they found that it miraculously grew lighter and lighter—until it was lightest of all on the highest passes. Once they were over the border, and into India, it returned to its former weight and they could carry it no further.

Because of this feat Dhardo Rimpoche regarded Tri-Ngawang Rimpoche and Nechung Rimpoche as heroes. Tri-Ngawang Rimpoche took a rented room on his own in Kalimpong and he and Dhardo Rimpoche resumed their friendship. Whenever one had any problem or difficulty the other would call to offer advice. When Tri-Ngawang came to the school he was bound to stay for at least three hours, during which time, in honour of the visit, Rimpoche would often give the children a three-hour break. Consequently he became known as 'Three-Hour Lama'.

During his two years in England as senior incumbent at the Hampstead Buddhist Vihara, Sangharakshita became something of a controversial figure. As he told Dhardo Rimpoche, he had not been able to heal the rift in the English Buddhist community. At first he had been popular with most people, but his outspokenness and unwillingness to be partisan to either of the warring camps had eventually alienated members of both. Despite this, he had come to the conclusion that there was great potential for spreading the Dharma in the West. When he returned to Kalimpong in 1967, therefore, he was on a farewell tour. Since leaving England, he had received a letter from the English Sangha Trust telling him that they did not want him to come back. He would have to make a fresh start. It had been one of Dhardo Rimpoche's earliest ideas that Sangharakshita should return to the West and teach there in his stead, and he now gave him his full support.

'I told Sangharakshita that he would be far more effective (in the West) than me or any other Buddhist teacher. In fact, as a Western *bhikkhu* he would be more effective than a hundred Tibetan lamas. I encouraged him to return to England telling him that I had confidence that he could do it.'

Within a year Sangharakshita had indeed struck out on his own and founded a Buddhist *order*. He did not forget Rimpoche, and was able, on occasion, to send donations to help him out. It was to be quite a few years before he would find himself able to help by any other means.

121

In encouraging Sangharakshita at this juncture, Rimpoche must have seen the parallel between his experience at Bodh Gaya and that of his disciple in London. However, in encouraging his disciple to enact his plans, Rimpoche knew that the parting would be lengthy and, perhaps, final. Before his departure in 1964, one last thing had seemed necessary to both: the bestowal of the highly auspicious practice of White Tara, the female Bodhisattva figure whose special qualities are wisdom and long life.

Rimpoche had himself received this initiation from the remarkable Pabongkapa Rimpoche. He was a small, barrel-chested man with a booming voice, famous for giving learned talks peppered with jokes and anecdotes. Dhardo Rimpoche had always been deeply affected by the teachings he had received from Pabongkapa.

White Tara is an enchanting, youthful girl, pure white and with hair 'the colour of the black Persian bee'. Adorned with jewels and silks, she sits in the adamantine position. In her left hand she holds a flower which blossoms by her right shoulder. On her forehead is an eye which is bright with the lustre of wisdom. On the soles of her feet and in the palms of her hands, 'wisdom eyes' shine out. All around, protecting those who contemplate her, she radiates a glorious, nimbus-like, many-coloured light.

13   In the Face of Adversity

*An old sage said: "Although the sun and moon are
shining brightly, the floating clouds cover them.
Although the clusters of orchids flourish, the autumn
wind wilts them." I would say that although the floating
clouds obscure the sun and moon, it is not for long;
although the autumn wind destroys them, the blossoms
will open again;... No matter how much evil arises, if
we steadfastly protect Buddhism over many long years,
the floating clouds will disappear, and the autumn wind
will stop.*[1]

Dhardo Rimpoche once remarked that only two things
interested him: to keep alive Tibetan culture, and to render
assistance to the poor. The ITBCI School attempted to do
both. At Drepung he had received the rarified education
of someone who was being prepared for a position of great
influence. Most of his present pupils came from very poor
homes and had parents who had received no education
whatsoever. But Buddhist practice perfumed his understanding of what education should be. Not long before his
death, he commented:

'The prime purpose of education, as I understand it,
is not just to learn from great books and hold a high
degree, but to get proper benefit from the learning.
Education must be meaningful, training a person to
be optimistic, upright, gentle, and helpful to
humanity.'[2]

[1] Dogen, *A Primer of Soto Zen*, trans. Masunaga, Routledge & Kegan
Paul, London, 1972
[2] *AFI Newsletter*, 1988, p.16

The children started to dress in Western clothes and applied themselves diligently to learning Hindi and English as well as their Tibetan subjects. But visitors to the school commented that they seemed to bear themselves with a grace and dignity which contrasted vividly with the squalor of the school buildings and the surrounding streets.

Jampel Kaldhen married and had a family. Dhardo Rimpoche came to treat Jampel's children as if they were his own. Whenever he was presented with offerings of fruit or sweetmeats, he would tell the children that they could eat any of them. When Mrs Kaldhen protested, Rimpoche would ask her to be lenient: 'We Tibetans have lost our country now; we should let our children eat while they are young and while there is still the opportunity. Otherwise, later, nothing is certain.' Zedhen, the eldest daughter, recalled that when she moved up to one of the senior schools, although Rimpoche had been desperate for money, he would give her a few sweets each day so that she would not feel left out among pupils from wealthier backgrounds.

The school sometimes seemed like an extension of the family. Rimpoche's presence pervaded all its activities. Whenever he returned from a business trip the children would rush to meet him and escort him down the steep steps which led from the road to the school. He would always stop and chat with them, placing his hand on their heads by way of blessing. One young boy with impaired speech was taken into his own household and given a place in a room with the Kaldhen family; each morning, Rimpoche taught the boy a wisdom mantra to help him improve his speech.

The school's activities were pervaded by the values which Dhardo Rimpoche espoused. The playground, which was situated on the roof of one of the huts, was often full of all sorts of mischief, but the children were often also to be seen practising steps they had learned from the dance-master. Each Tibetan region has its own distinctive dances. These were all kept alive in the school. On special occasions, the regional costumes would be unpacked from the store-room and the musical instruments tuned up so that the pupils could display their talents. Sometimes the special twelve foot snow-lion would make an appearance and, in a show of remarkable skill, it danced as if it were truly alive. Quieter, and demanding more concentration, was the art class where the pupils learned the principles of Tibetan religious painting. They learned how to prepare the canvasses and gild statues, how to use a few animal hairs to make the finest of brushes, and how to take a pinch of dull pigment and grind it into a brilliant natural paint.

By the 1970s, the shanties which housed the school hung precipitously close to a ravine. During each monsoon season the ravine was driven deeper and wider by the swollen water-course at its base. The world of Tibetan Buddhism is suffused with symbolism, and now the water-course seemed to be mocking the school with a metaphor for its financial plight. Each year the school had been forced to dig deeper and deeper into its meagre reserves until it was hanging on the brink of disaster. One new building had been erected a few years previously, housing a room for Rimpoche and some extra class-rooms. But the school's intake had increased to 240. There was barely enough money to support the orphans and boarders who slept in rows of rough and ready bunks in the drafty basement of the wooden shanties. The teachers' salary was Rs200, about £11, per month—about a tenth of what they would have received at government schools. Rimpoche was dreadfully ashamed to ask the teachers to live on this salary.

In desperation, he hunted through his trunks, pawning

or selling anything to tide the school over. There was a 'Tibetan Heritage' display, containing a few ancient silver and copper coins; this was sold to service the urgent needs of the present. Rimpoche regularly picked pieces of wood out of the gutter and carried them back for the fire. He picked up bamboo canes which had been used for toy sword-fights, collected plastic bags, string, wrapping paper—anything which might save spending a rupee.

One day in 1977, two of Sangharakshita's students appeared at the gate of the ITBCI School. Rimpoche had seen neither Sangharakshita nor any of his disciples for over ten years and was delighted by this unexpected visit. They were Englishmen who went by the Buddhist names, Surata and Lokamitra, which Sangharakshita had given them. For them, Dhardo Rimpoche had hitherto been no more than an exotic name from their teacher's past. But they were attending a Yoga course in Poona, and Sangharakshita had asked them to find out how Dhardo Rimpoche and his school were faring. Sangharakshita especially wanted to know about its financial position.

It was not long before Lokamitra discovered that the school was virtually without money; he was struck by Dhardo Rimpoche's sincerity and the valiant efforts he had been making to keep the school going. The school needed £3,000 urgently and Lokamitra pledged himself to raise it. He returned to England to attend a convention of Sangharakshita's 'Western Buddhist Order' and was able to collect £500 on the spot; in the following months, the Order raised the balance, saving the school from ruin. Rimpoche was overjoyed.

In 1978, Lokamitra moved to Poona, in western India, to work among the ex-Untouchable Buddhist followers of Dr Ambedkar. The tiny rented room from which he operated soon proved far too small, for at times he found himself teaching the Dharma to people in their hundreds.

Usually the venue was a piece of waste ground, or a back street in the slum districts where most of Poona's 300,000 Buddhists lived. Lokamitra needed a base. He also saw that his Buddhist work would have to be accompanied by social work, to help relieve the dreadful poverty of the people he was teaching. He hoped to create a medical centre and resource centre, and drew up plans for a building which would cost thousands of pounds to construct. The Western Buddhist Order therefore set up a charity, called Aid For India, to raise this money, and volunteers took to the streets of British cities to ask people to help with the work. The charity proved far more successful than had been hoped and, within a year, it had raised covenanted donations worth several hundreds of thousands of pounds.

In 1982, one of the charity's trustees, Dharmachari Nagabodhi, took the opportunity to visit Dhardo Rimpoche and he, too, was shocked by the appalling conditions of the school. He had a frank talk with Rimpoche and asked him how much it would cost to build all the accommodation and class-rooms he needed, how much for maintenance and repairs, and how much for teachers' salaries. When the sum was worked out it was surprisingly little by AFI standards, just £35,000. It was not difficult to persuade the trustees of the charity to take on the support of the school. Although the charity's first priority had to be the raising of funds for Lokamitra's work in Poona, in 1985 a dozen people spent eight weeks tramping the London streets, knocking on suburban doors and asking for donations for the ITBCI School. The appeal raised £150,000, enough to cater for the needs of the school over seven years, and more than Rimpoche had mustered in over thirty.

By the time the first funds were received in 1986, it was clear to Rimpoche that, at last, the responsibility for fund-raising was no longer being borne by himself alone, and that the severe financial worries which had plagued the school since its inception were at an end. He later commented, 'People feel that life is short. Because of this, instead of working for others, they just try to acquire wealth for themselves. If we live in this way, we become isolated. Our lives become like bubbles on the surface of water. But people can be inspired by action. If they see something is happening, they start to give.... If you work hard in the right way, it will spread like light.'

Jampel Kaldhen worked with a local architect to design a beautiful new building on the old site, and construction work soon began. Each day, after his dinner, Rimpoche would inspect the site, stepping around the building material and quietly murmuring his approval. By 1988 the shanties had been demolished and a beautiful two-storeyed building, complete with a miniature golden pagoda-roof, had taken its place. By 1990 two new blocks had been completed. The basement housed dormitories for the twenty-eight boarders and on the ground and first floors there were seven class-rooms, plus a few rooms for resident teachers and for some of Jampel Kaldhen's family. His wooden house had been knocked down in preparation for a fourth building designed to complete the quadrangle. Finally, there was a small shrine-room, and a beautifully decorated stage for music and dance opened onto the central courtyard.

Members of the Western Buddhist Order started to visit Rimpoche in increasing numbers. When I made my first visit in 1986, he doubled up with his head in his hands and groaned when I had requested initiation. He explained that since Sangharakshita had left he had given only one other initiation to a Westerner, and wondered if I would have the ability to receive one. But, whatever conclusion he reached about that, he was very happy to teach

8. A Festival at the Bhutanese Palace – Rimpoche, centre, wearing tall lama hat

9. Below: With Sangharakshita, *1967*

11. Rimpoche presents offering scarf to Dalai Lama on his visit to the ITBCI School, *1975*

12. Pupils in front of new school block, *1990*

10. Opposite: Rimpoche in the Bhutanese Palace, *mid 1950s*

13. Rimpoche performing Fire-puja at Yi Ga Choling, *Nov 1989*

14. The upper chamber of the cremation stupa

members of the Western Buddhist Order. He remarked, 'I find that these people work very hard, and their interest in Buddhism is genuine. Tibetan people here do not show enough concern.' When asked how he viewed his relation to Sangharakshita's pupils, his feelings were clear. He said, 'I do not make any distinction between my own disciples and those of Sangharakshita.'

Although many other lamas had passed through Kalimpong, Rimpoche had always been very popular among the ordinary people. When the school started to flourish, their respect for him was simply confirmed. But within ecclesiastical and governmental circles Rimpoche had been almost forgotten. Suddenly, after thirty-six years, old Dhardo Tulku had, through quiet persistence, brought to completion the first school worthy of the Tibetan community. It was one of the very few anywhere in India run by and for Tibetans, and, so far as I can tell, the only one not limited by sponsorship from Indian Government funding. Furthermore, every year increasing numbers of Western Buddhists were coming to meet him—rather than visiting Dharamsala or Dalhousie where the Dalai Lama and other noted lamas resided.

Throughout the sixties and much of the seventies, the local Gelugpa monasteries had relied on teachings from top ecclesiastical dignitaries and gifted lamas who stayed in Kalimpong after fleeing Tibet. But most of these had long since left. There were now very few incarnate lamas empowered to pass on the higher initiations of the Tantra, and no *geshes* of the Lharampa grade. Ventul Tulku, one of the two remaining Gelugpa *tulkus* who still lives in Kalimpong, said that the Westerners' visits awoke the monastic community to the fact that they had a remarkable lama right on their doorstep. Most, to be fair, had settled in Kalimpong long after Rimpoche, and it was perhaps natural for them to regard him primarily as the lama who ran the school; but it now became clear that the school was really a natural outflow of Dhardo Rimpoche's profound spiritual inspiration.

The monks invited him to conduct monastic ordination ceremonies and, in 1989, asked him to give a full month's teachings in a large hall in Kalimpong. Rimpoche so exceeded their expectations that they lamented not having appreciated his capacities before. He bestowed initiations of protection upon the several hundred monks and lay people present, and concluded the session by giving a select few the initiation of Vajrabhairava, 'Diamond-Terror', which he had been given in Dhartsendo by his first teacher, Jampa Rimpoche. During the days of this initiation he was immersed in transmitting his experience of over sixty years of daily visualization of this figure. Lama Anagarika Govinda saw a deep significance in this depiction of the Wrathful Manjushri:

> '(He) represents the double nature of man who shares his physical nature, his instincts, drives, and passions, with the animals, and his spiritual nature with the divine forces of the universe. As a physical being he is mortal, as a spiritual being he is immortal. If his intellect is combined with his animal nature, demonic forces are born, while the intellect guided by his spiritual nature produces divine qualities.'[1]

Dhardo Rimpoche's long years of work and practice were coming to fruition. It was starting to be recognized that the quietness of his achievements was part of their strength, and that everything came out of his practice of Buddhism. On the façade of his new school building was painted a cast of the school symbol. Here, two deer hold up the Buddha's 'Wheel of Truth'; above flies a banner showing

[1] *The Way of the White Clouds,* p.244

an eagle-lion, a fish-otter, and a crocodile-conch. These are the hybrid animals representing the peace and harmony which prevailed when the Buddha was alive. Topmost are three radiant jewels. A golden jewel represents the Buddha, the exemplar of wisdom and compassion; a blue jewel represents the Dharma, the teaching he imparted and the Truth he discovered; and a red jewel represents the Sangha, the community of those who, throughout time and across space, tread the Buddha's Path.

14 The Last Pilgrimage

The time has come to go; like a traveller, I must be on
my way.
My joy in dying has been well earned:
It is greater than all the wealth in the ocean a merchant
may have won, or
The godlike power of having conquered armies, or
The bliss found in meditation.

Now that the connection with this life has lost its karmic
power,
Do not lament about this beggar who died happily and
unattached,
But constantly pray (that he may be with you in spirit).[1]

Towards the end of 1989, one of Sangharakshita's disciples had a dream in which Rimpoche appeared surrounded by numerous eclipsed suns in a sky filled with scorpions. This was regarded as a 'big' dream, and one which Rimpoche thought should not be taken lightly. He was entering the seventy-third year of his life, an age which Tibetan astrology considers inauspicious for men. This was a time for engaging in meritorious acts whose ripening fruit might have a strengthening effect. Rimpoche's health had not been good in recent years and so, before it might decline any further, he decided to undertake a long-cherished project: he would make a pilgrimage to the holy places of Nepal. By contemplating the places in which the Buddha and the great Buddhist teachers had once stood, and by

---

[1] Longchanpa, 'Now That I Come to Die', *Crystal Mirror* V, Dharma Publishing, 1977

making offerings to them, he hoped to establish the necessary spiritual resources to sustain him through the coming year.

A pilgrimage is a journey into a world of myth. Events which have seemed to be shut away behind the closed doors along time's long corridor become as alive and as fresh as if they had happened yesterday. To the pilgrim, everyday reality and imagination are no longer separate: a shape, a noise, an unexpected meeting, can be charged with significance, becoming a symbol of something 'beyond us, yet ourselves'. One dwells more intensely on how one acts within one's environment, and on the effect of that environment upon oneself. Such intense concentration, coupled with reflection on the life of the Buddha and on the lives of the great sages who followed him, brings about a deep sense of faith which flowers as inspiration. The pilgrim gives himself to the pilgrimage with body, speech, and mind, and the fruits of his devotion manifest as virtue. He comes to feel blessed; in the traditional phrase, he feels 'richly endowed'.

Rimpoche set off in January 1990, attended by Jampel Kaldhen, with his wife, two sons, two daughters, and a grandchild. In Kathmandu, Gangchen Rimpoche generously supplied the party with a jeep, two monks to act as guides, and food for the month-long journey. There had been plans for Rimpoche to spend a month at Gangchen Rimpoche's monastery in Kathmandu in order to deliver teachings and initiations to the monks. But the astrological portents were unfavourable and he arrived in Kathmandu later than had been hoped. There were nevertheless reception meals in various supporters' houses, blessings to be imparted, temples to be visited, and teachings to be expounded at Gangchen Rimpoche's monastery. But after just a few days the party set off across Nepal.

The journey lasted a full month, during which time
Dhardo Rimpoche took only a few hours rest. The party
visited the great Buddhist *stupas* of Bauddha and
Swayambhu. As he travelled he gave money to provide
new coats of whitewash for the monuments; a number of
Gelugpa monasteries were given money to repaint their
façades; and he made a small donation to every monk.
Each beggar who approached was also given something.
Eventually, Wangpo, one of Jampel Kaldhen's sons, piped
up: 'Rimpoche! You can't give to every beggar—how
many are there in the world?' But Rimpoche replied: 'You
don't know what I'm doing. Just let me give.'

And so the practice continued throughout the
pilgrimage. There were visits to the major holy places in
the Kathmandu valley, and to smaller and less accessible
shrines. Often, Rimpoche strode energetically ahead of his
attendants, but sometimes the effort was too much and he
had to be carried pick-a-back by his secretary. One visit
involved a long drive to a secluded spot, a walk of several
hours over very rough terrain, and, finally, a climb over
large boulders and up a steep hillside to a hidden cave.
There, the great eleventh century Enlightened master,
Milarepa, had lived for several years and, inspired by the
depths of his meditative experience, composed many of
his beautiful songs. Eventually, on reaching the cave, the
necessary rituals were carried out and the descent made
in growing darkness. Everyone was amazed at the deter-
mination and hidden strength displayed by Rimpoche. On
a hillside north of Kathmandu, another cave contained a
statue of great beauty and simplicity—which was said to
have manifested spontaneously from the rock. It was as if
there was no place to which Dhardo Rimpoche would not
go. Indeed, the more visits he made, the happier he seemed
to become.

At last, the party returned to Kathmandu for a meeting

with Gangchen Rimpoche and to impart further teachings to his disciples. Since Rimpoche had already given blessings and basic initiations, Ganchen Rimpoche requested that he now give some more advanced teachings. Dhardo Rimpoche explained that several of his Western disciples were already waiting for him in Kalimpong, but said he would stay for two more days. Ganchen Rimpoche therefore asked him to give the Vajrabhairava teachings once again. Rimpoche stipulated that the bestowal of so high an initiation should not be public but only for those properly qualified to receive it.

Over forty initiates squeezed into a room in Gangchen Rimpoche's house. For two days Dhardo Rimpoche instructed them in the visualization and invocation of the wrathful figure whose primordial power breaks through all conceivable obstacles to the attainment of the Goal.

By this time he was several days behind schedule, but was nevertheless unsure whether to return by road or by air. After thinking the matter over, he performed a divination by throwing a 'mo'. All indications suggested that he should return by road, and so he took the rough, bumpy road, bounded by precipitous ravines, back to Kalimpong, arriving late on Thursday, 22 February. Everyone was exhausted by the journey and Rimpoche had a slight bowel upset. He therefore spent the Friday resting and planned to receive his Western visitors on the Saturday morning. On Friday morning, however, a good friend was suddenly taken ill; Rimpoche immediately went to his bedside to comfort and encourage him. Before the night was out, his friend was dead.

The next morning Rimpoche rose a little later than usual. He dressed and was engaged in the ritual of cleaning his teeth while chanting mantras and visualizing himself as Vajrabhairava. Suddenly, a blinding pain shot through his head.

When Rimpoche called out in agony, Jampel came rushing to his aid. Seeing that something terrible had happened he immediately sent for a doctor. The Western-trained doctor diagnosed a stroke and recommended that Rimpoche should go to hospital without delay. But Rimpoche had never been to hospital and was strong enough to insist that he wanted to be treated in his own house, by his own people, and surrounded by his Buddha statues and *thangkas*. Rimpoche's Tibetan doctor, Khu-shok Lhawang-la, was called and he too prescribed medicines.

In Kalimpong and at Yi Ga Choling Gompa, *pujas* were held to invoke beneficent forces on Rimpoche's behalf. A local painter was commissioned to paint a *thangka* of White Tara within a specified twenty-four hour period, so that Rimpoche might be protected by her gift of long life.

Over the next two weeks Rimpoche's progress was monitored by both doctors, and he seemed to be regaining his health. Slowly his strength returned and he was able to walk with support. But Lhawang-la was still concerned. An important pulse was not yet normal and a Tibetan astrologer indicated that the end of March would be the most critical time of all; if Rimpoche survived until then, the crisis would be past. The astrologer urged Lhawang-la not to leave prematurely.

During the third week of March, the Western-trained doctor announced that Rimpoche was out of the critical phase; indeed, he was able to walk about unaided. Rimpoche now called an astrologer and asked him to look at the signs in his chart. The astrologer expressed grave concern since 'the sun was facing water' until the end of the month. This, along with other indications, seemed very bad. To counter this ominous configuration, the astrologer and Tibetan doctor ordered four sets of *pujas* to be performed. All the Gelugpa monks in Kalimpong gathered and requested Rimpoche to attend a long-life *puja*. It was a long ritual, but he looked much better by the end.

Rimpoche's behaviour from this point onwards tells its own story. He ordered new silks to be sewn up for some of his ritual implements which had become worn. He arranged his library of rare books, and re-arranged the *thangkas* in his room so that he could meditate on them whilst lying down. Two *thangkas*, whose special meditation theme was death, were then hung at the foot of his bed where he could look directly at them. By their side was a rather poor specimen of the art, but it had been painted by his dear friend Tri-Ngawang Rimpoche, 'Three-Hour Lama', who had died a few years previously. Finally he gave some rosaries, which he had bought in Nepal, to Jampel's family.

Friday's examination revealed that the crucial pulse had returned to normal. Lhawang-la was satisfied that Rimpoche had fully recovered. For the first time in weeks he ate a hearty breakfast, with several large pieces of Tibetan bread and a full measure of tea. He told everyone that the bread tasted wonderful—almost the best he had ever eaten. During the day he left his first-floor room and crossed to the new school block and climbed to the flat roof above the second floor in order to look out over Kalimpong. Although he walked virtually unaided, Tashi Dorje, the dance-master, would not let him go alone. Rimpoche drank in the sunshine and admired the view. He declared that he had been lucky to live in Kalimpong, for it was so beautiful. Laughing, he re-arranged his upper robe and said to Tashi Dorje, 'Look, this is how Ministers walk in Lhasa!' and proceeded to mimic their characteristic, magisterial stroll. Below, in the school courtyard, a number of teachers had rushed out from their class-rooms to catch a glimpse of Rimpoche on the roof. They could see that Rimpoche was well and strong and that he looked happy. They waved up to him and many of their eyes filled with tears of relief. One school-child was so delighted that she darted out of the school gate, ran home and announced to her mother 'Rimpoche is recovered!'

But for those who spent the most time with Rimpoche, the relief was tempered by a concern raised by some of his recent actions. That morning, on rising, he had ordered Dorje and Lhawang-la: 'Fold away the extra blankets. They are not needed.' They were confused, for the nights were still very cold. But, no, Rimpoche would listen to no objections, and ordered that the blankets and extra clothing should be returned to their storage chest. Tashi Dorje pleaded with Rimpoche not to speak in such a way—it was inauspicious.

When evening came, Rimpoche asked Jampel to fetch the text of a *puja* concerned with death and dying. Jampel protested that Rimpoche was still only just recovering and that the *puja* was far too long and demanding. Rimpoche insisted that if Jampel would not fetch it, he would do so himself. What else could Jampel do but comply? Rimpoche proceeded with the ritual in his room while, downstairs, the others listened to his voice—which now seemed stronger than ever as it boomed out cycle after cycle of the long text. There was no faltering and there were no mistakes throughout the entire, complex ritual.

Rimpoche's chanting died away; he called out to Wangpo to bring his father. Knowing Jampel had been unfailing in his service to Rimpoche for weeks on end—and was virtually exhausted by the strain, Wangpo was reluctant to disturb him. But Rimpoche would listen to no objections: Wangpo was to fetch his father immediately. Jampel, of course, came running. Rimpoche wanted him to write an important letter immediately. It was dark and, because the power supply was so low, there was barely enough light to see. Jampel tried to object, but Rimpoche exclaimed, 'For what other purpose have I made little table lamps, with my own hands, if not for using in poor light?' But it was so late, argued Jampel. Exasperated, Rimpoche said that it was of the utmost importance that a letter be sent off to two members of the Western Buddhist Order, Subhuti and Lokamitra, who had visited him the previous day but whom he had not been able to see. Rimpoche felt it imperative that he write, apologizing for not receiving them, and explaining that he had not even known of their presence. Jampel assured Rimpoche that he would write without fail the next morning and Rimpoche seemed satisfied with his assurance.

However, there were still many other things on his mind. Jampel was to bring paper and pen. Almost sinking under the burden of his concern, Jampel sighed a protest; but, no, Jampel just did not know what was important. He, Rimpoche, did. Resigned to the task, Jampel went off and returned along with his wife and daughter, Zedhen. He was carrying a tape recorder which, as it turned out, suited the needs of what followed much better.

Rimpoche announced that it was now time for Jampel to ask all the questions he had never before asked. Nothing else could be more important at this juncture. Jampel insisted that Rimpoche was better now and that he would live until he was eighty. 'No, no,' Rimpoche playfully replied, 'I have prayed to live to eighty-five, so I am sure I will live at least that long.' But becoming fully serious again, he insisted that Jampel must ask his questions now.

Cautiously, Jampel asked, what should happen when Rimpoche died. Two special *pujas* should be performed, Rimpoche said. Not the usual ones but the Vajradakini *puja* and Vajrabhairava fire-*puja*. On no account was he to be cremated like a high lama, trussed up in meditation posture. He wanted to be cremated like an ordinary person in 'lying posture', as Tri-Ngawang Rimpoche had been. He had carried out the death wishes of 'Three-Hour Lama' by cremating him in this way—and had been severely criticized for it; people had even said that he was mean-spirited. But Rimpoche knew that his friend had entrusted him with his death-wishes, and he was not willing to compromise them. He hoped that the same might be done for him. As for a memorial reliquary, while in Nepal he had especially appreciated the gold and silver *stupa* of his late friend, Serkong Tulku. If there was enough money, Jampel was to make one like that. If not, the usual statue in which his ashes might be placed would suffice.

'What about the school?' Jampel asked. It was still held in Dhardo Rimpoche's name, so he insisted that it should be transferred as soon as possible to a set of trustees. He especially wanted the school to continue to have a link with Sangharakshita's Western Buddhist Order. The trustees should include at least one foreign Order member, two from Poona, and two members of the Tibetan community. Rimpoche continued to talk for almost an hour, his quiet, steady voice ranging over a variety of subjects.

But the crucial question was still to come, the one which Jampel feared would pose the greatest difficulty. What about Rimpoche's next rebirth? Would there be a fourteenth Dhardo Tulku? Jampel knew that Rimpoche had already said several times that, as far as he was concerned, he would not leave instructions about his rebirth. If he had the power of choice over his new birthplace he would choose somewhere suitable and would not require the additional help of 'official' recognition. If he did not have such powers, then whatever directions he left would be worse than useless. The wrong boy might be 'discovered', which would be disastrous.

Jampel pleaded with him: 'But Rimpoche what will we do without you? What will the school do without you?' Zedhen and Jampel's wife joined in the entreaties and, after some time, Rimpoche relented a little. If there ever were to be another Dhardo Tulku, he said, only Jampel would be able to recognize him. Jampel was more alarmed than ever by this prospect. How could he ever recognize a boy as being the genuine Dhardo Tulku?

'What have I brought you all this way from Tibet for?' Rimpoche replied. 'If *you* don't know me by this time, who else will? If there is to be any recognition you must do it. The boy must have the same qualities as I have. I don't have ordinary feelings—I have continual compassion for people. Only a boy with those qualities will do.'

When Jampel went out on an errand, Rimpoche joked with his wife and Zedhen. 'You think I'm weak and have lost all my strength. I've not!' He took Mrs Kaldhen's hand in his and squeezed it until she cried out. 'It hurts—I believe you!' Zedhen also had to try—with the same result. When Jampel returned and had his hand squeezed, he too cried out in pain, but Rimpoche was not fooled and told him he was faking. There were laughs all round.

Late at night, Dhardo Rimpoche performed his daily *puja* for the dead. Though the hour was late and the day had been long, his voice rang strong and clear as he chanted the words. At one point in this ritual, spoonfuls of offerings are burnt for the sake of the dead. Rimpoche's habit was to spoon five heaps onto the charcoal fire; but on this night there were seven. As the offerings burned on the fire, the room filled with the scent of their smoke; he asked that the windows and doors be flung open to let out the aromas, so they might spread into the night.

At some time after eleven o'clock, Rimpoche lay down in his bed, watched over by Jampel and his wife, who slept on mats next to him. He soon fell asleep, but awoke just after one o'clock to use the latrine bucket. Jampel Kaldhen helped him and then Rimpoche settled back in bed. As Jampel was about to leave with the bucket, Rimpoche gave a slight groan and his head dropped the last few inches onto the bed.

Mrs Kaldhen called out, 'Rimpoche. Are you asleep so soon?' But there was no reply.

They rushed to him to find that his pulse was fading. His breath could scarcely be felt. They sent for Khu-Shok Lhawang-la and he came almost instantly. He studied all the pulses but, after a few minutes, he could feel none, and announced that at 1.15 a.m, on Saturday 24 March, Dhardo Rimpoche had died.

When a lama who is an adept at meditation dies, it is said that his mind rests in meditative absorption for several hours after the body has ceased to live. Only when he is content that his meditation is complete does he leave the body. At that time, it is said, red and white fluid leaves the nostrils. Lhawang-la accordingly told Jampel that the body must not be disturbed, on any account, until the fluids were seen. Jampel Kaldhen sat silently, with his wife, stunned and grief-stricken, watching by the body— which did not seem dead, even though Rimpoche was no longer alive. As the sun rose outside the room, the fluids ran from his nose. Jampel called Lhawang-la, who announced that Dhardo Rimpoche had left his body. That body now took on the colourless and waxy features of a corpse.

15 The Wheel and the Diamond

At such a time of mourning as this,
Of themselves [unaided] the flames burst out,
Assuming shapes of the Eight Auspicious Emblems and
*   the Seven Precious Insignia,*
And various beauteous objects of religious offering.[1]

A few days before Rimpoche's death, I had an exceptionally beautiful dream. Rimpoche called me to him and
asked to hold my hand for a few moments. I offered it as
though for a handshake, but he did not want it like that;
he wanted to take it gently and enfold it in the warmth of
his own. As he did so, he breathed, 'We will meet again.'
I woke, feeling very much at peace and in no way anxious
to see him. As the days wore on I had no doubt that I had
been in his mind; in fact Jampel later related that he had
repeatedly asked where I was and if I was coming. Jampel
had kept stalling, saying that I would come later, when he
was better.

Word of Dhardo Rimpoche's death spread quickly
through Kalimpong, through the Buddhist community,
and among the Gelugpa sangha across India. There was
widespread grief and a dawning sense of how remarkable
his life had been. Gelugpa monks and Rimpoches arrived
in Kalimpong to present offerings, and to enact the
elaborate *pujas* and ceremonies which follow the death of
an important lama. These ceremonies commemorate the
life which has passed, and symbolically accompany the
lama's consciousness as it passes through the *bardo*, or
intermediate state, which is held to follow death.

[1] Evans-Wentz, *Tibet's Great Yogi Milarepa*, p.287

Lhawang-la performed the ritual purification of the body, and preparations were made to cremate it. The visiting lamas insisted that Dhardo Tulku must be bound and cremated in sitting meditation posture; Jampel and his family, supported by Ventul Tulku, were adamant that Rimpoche's wishes should be honoured, and that he should be burnt prostrate. But it was held that he was a most 'highly attained lama', and tradition insisted that, whatever his own views, he must be cremated in meditation posture. The assembled monks and lamas had their way.

Thus it was that on the day of the cremation, some seven days after his death, Rimpoche's body was installed in state. It was wound in cloth, seated in meditation posture, dressed in gorgeous, gold-embroidered, red Tantric robes, and topped with a Bodhisattva crown. Former disciples and pupils from the school streamed past to present their offerings. The body was then placed on a palanquin and carried through the town. Hundreds of people swarmed around to get a last glimpse of their teacher, and to throw their offering scarves. Soon the palanquin was swathed deep in white cotton, silk, and muslin. Then, to the accompaniment of trumpets and cymbals from red-robed monks, it climbed the winding mountain roads up towards the misty heights of Yi Ga Choling Monastery.

The cavalcade stopped many times on the mountain roads leading from Kalimpong, allowing the country people to pay their respects. It was therefore not until mid-morning that it arrived in Ghoom. I had heard the news while I was still in Kathmandu and had come as swiftly as I could, along with my travelling companion, Yashomitra, to be in time for the cremation.

At Ghoom, the long track to the *gompa* had been lined with people since sunrise, each carrying a bundle of incense wrapped in white offering scarves. Some of them were tossing juniper and aromatic herbs onto little charcoal burners so that their fragrant fumes mingled with the mist that poured down the freezing mountainside. As the jeeps hauled their way up the rough and rocky track, incense smoke washed over them and more scarves were thrown. A group of red-hatted monks from the neighbouring monastery of the Shakyapa school put their trumpets to their mouths, puffed out their cheeks until their noses sank out of sight, and rent the air with the piercing wail of their instruments. Hearing this, the boys on the roof of Yi Ga Choling Gompa let out blasts from massive, growling horns. This set the crowd in motion like a vast swarm of bees. The jeep bearing the palanquin, topped with a swirling yellow royal umbrella, crawled into the compound as the crowd trailed in its wake. Scarves flew in the air, thick as snow, until neither the body nor the palanquin could be seen.

The throne was taken down from the jeep and carried on a final circuit of the monastery. Back in the courtyard, it was placed on a vast silk-covered table where the very last offering scarves were presented. The final three scarves were offered by myself and Yashomitra. We had brought three especially long, pure white silk scarves, embossed with auspicious signs and mantras. We offered the first on behalf of Sangharakshita, and placed it over Rimpoche's lap; we placed the second on the throne behind Rimpoche, on behalf of the men's wing of the Western Buddhist Order.

The body was then taken behind a screen to a large, hastily-built *stupa* that had been constructed on the side of a hill. A hole gaped in the side of the vase-shaped chamber, and the body was passed through. When Rimpoche's body was inside, the *stupa* was sealed. Final decorations were now hung around it and I presented the third scarf, on behalf of the women's wing of the Order.

Ventul Rimpoche, who had been given the task of heading the funeral rites, led the convocation of twenty monks in the chanting of the ritual. First came a short Vajradakini rite, after which the youngest novice poked a fire-brand through each of four holes in the 'basement' of the *stupa*. Thus began a long Yamantaka fire-*puja*. During this ritual the monks visualized Rimpoche in the form of bull-headed Vajrabhairava seated inside a vast jewelled palace surrounded by twelve mysterious attendants—all of whom were given sacred offerings. In the wrathful form of the bull-headed demon he is the conqueror of Yama, Lord of Death. Vajrabhairava recognizes that death, too, is *Shunyata*—the diamond-like wisdom of the *vajra* cuts through the illusion of life and death in the Wheel of Existence.

Dark brown smoke began to pour from the top of the *stupa* as Ventul Rimpoche blessed various offerings which, one by one, were poured in through access points at the cardinal points. He offered ghee, sesame seed, mustard seed, grasses, and pulses. Smoke and mist poured under the canvas awning where the monks were sitting, and tears poured from their eyes. But the ritual carried on unabated to its conclusion, whereupon the younger monks ran off spluttering and coughing, to be revived by deep draughts of tea. The holes at the base and on the sides were now carefully sealed; thus the *stupa* was to remain for five days.

During those days, my mind was filled with memories of him. I recalled my first meeting, and his attempts at English when we were left alone for a while—Jampel Kaldhen and his family were watching, of all things, the English FA Cup Final in the next room. Rimpoche asked, 'You like football?' I told him that I never watched it. Then, to my surprise, making fighting gestures, he said, 'Other one—bad one!' I thought he meant wrestling. 'No, other one.' Did he mean boxing? 'Yes boxy, bad one; many hit head, many hit bad. Life not long, life small. Bad one! Bad one!'

I recalled my second visit, along with three other Dharmacharis. Rimpoche had teased us by saying that it was now time to test us; *we* should ask questions, and our quality would be revealed.

I recalled the great attention which Rimpoche gave me whenever I spoke. I thought of his meticulousness in opening the gifts I had brought him; every piece of string was slowly untied and the paper gingerly unwrapped—treated, in fact, with as much care as the present itself. In a back room were numerous bundles of coloured plastic raffia which he hung on hooks, a testament to his thrift. There were even piles of ordinary bamboo canes stacked in corners in this back room—just in case they might come in useful.

I recalled the rope high above his shrine, laden with offering scarves. Each one had been offered to him—and he had then offered it to the Buddhas and Bodhisattvas.

On the fifth day, a ceremony took place in the course of which the *stupa* was reopened. The bones and ashes were to be taken back to Kalimpong and settled in a shrine atop the school, but before this could be done, each bone had to be examined for special marks and signs which might indicate Rimpoche's degree of attainment. For himself, he had never set much store by such signs; he preferred to form an impression of a person's degree of spirituality from the way they lived their life. But the disinterment served a further function; in preparing the *stupa*, a man-dala, or symbolic circle, had been drawn in the sand with the symbols of five Buddhas. A *vajra* had been inscribed at the centre of the mandala, and around it were a lotus of compassion, a sword of wisdom, flaming Refuge jewels, the Wheel of Truth—or Dharmachakra, and eight more smaller *vajras*. It was necessary to examine these to see which of them had survived incineration; they might give some indication as to the birthplace of the next Dhardo Tulku.

It was therefore with a degree of trepidation that Ventul Rimpoche opened the *stupa*; I was directed to come close, to see and photograph the exact position of the remains. The first thing I saw was a clay urn beneath the grill upon which the body had been placed. Beyond that, all I could make out in the darkness was a mass of charred ash and bone. But once my eyes became accustomed to the light I looked up and, there, lodged in the grill, were the remains of the pelvis and spinal column, and Rimpoche's complete skull.

With the greatest of care, Ventul Rimpoche and his helpers picked up the loose bones piece by piece, down to the smallest fragment. These were placed in a polythene bag which was in turn placed inside an orange silk bag. Pieces of debris of dubious origin were put in another bag, and ordinary ash in a third. When this painstaking process was complete, the urn was removed and its contents treated in the same way. Finally, the base was swept clean. Where the urn had stood could now be seen the gentle dome of an ash-smeared metal plate. I had no idea what the significance of this might be, but Ventul Rimpoche and his helpers took such tremendous care in lifting it that it was clear that whatever lay beneath must be of great significance.

As I crouched with Ventul Rimpoche in the dim and charred interior of the *stupa*—which only days before we had imagined as the Diamond Palace of Vajrabhairava—the metal plate was removed. The base was covered in sand, and I could just distinguish the remains of the mandala which had been drawn in it. The main outlines of the mandala could still be seen, but only two of the thirteen symbols now remained.

There was much exclaiming, pushing, and jostling as people tried to get a clear view of the mystic symbols. Ventul Rimpoche asked me to photograph the mandala with great care, from different angles, and with two cameras. Directly east, by the rim of the mandala, was the Dharmachakra, the Wheel of Truth which the Buddha set turning two-and-a-half millennia ago. In the centre, pointing east-west, was the clear symbol of Akshobya Buddha, 'The Immovable One', the diamond-sceptre of the lamas, a symbol of the magisterial command exercised by the indestructible power of Reality.

I had visited Dhardo Rimpoche twice in his school and spent almost all of the available time with him. I had spent many hours listening to his voice on tape, and many hours watching his face on video recordings. I had reflected on what he had said about his life, and I had spent days and weeks engrossed in researching it. Above all, I had spent many hours dwelling on photographs of him as they lay on my shrine. The diamond-sceptre and the Wheel of Truth had been his most favoured symbols—they even appeared on the letter-heading of his personal note-paper; their appearance in the *stupa* seemed to be telling me something about his life.

I cannot adequately describe my experience as I crouched within the cremation chamber. While looking down at the symbols of the mandala I could feel Rimpoche's compelling presence, which seemed to stare through the empty sockets of his skull, burning into my back, challenging me. It was as if he was saying: 'Try to meet your end like this!'

May the teaching and example of his life never fade.

The Harmonious Sound of the Sage of Truth

Herein is contained a prayer for swift rebirth entitled:
'The Harmonious Sound of the Sage of Truth'

OM SVASTI

I make obeisance to the unfailing three precious jewels:
To the Buddha-body, adorned and bedecked by major
    and minor marks,
And perfected in both renunciation and realization,
To the Doctrine (leading to) the path of cessation, which
    is enunciated in sixty harmonious aspects,
And to the sublime assembly, which is endowed with
    eight kinds of liberated awareness.

I pray to the sun of the doctrine which illuminates
The excellent [*legs*] expressions of the Conquerors whose
    enlightened activity is a great wave, effortlessly and
    spontaneously accomplished,
In the presence of those fortunate [*bzang*] ones to be
    trained
In the great grove of lotus flowers which is the Sage's
    [*thub*] teaching [*bstan*].[1]

O Venerable Guru, whose Buddha-mind embodies all
    the perfected innermost intentions of the conquerors
    of the three times without exception,
You are unrivalled in maintaining, protecting, and
    expanding this profound exegetical tradition of the
    conquerors, endowed with excellent intelligence.

---

[1] This verse is a play on Rimpoche's monastic name, Thubten Legsang
(*thub.bstan.legs.bzang*)

Although there have indeed been many truly proud
  sasanadhara,
It is extremely sad at this time when the liberating
  career of a son who maintains the legacy of a father is
  rarely cultivated,
Owing to the lowly fortune of living beings in an evil
  age.

Transmitting each distinct exegetical teaching of the
  different learned and accomplished masters of the
  past who were impartial, such as Lord Manjushri and
  Mahakarunika who came before,
You are accordingly unrivalled in maintaining the
  excellent tradition.

You are assuredly a Lord and Refuge who dispels the
  unbearable torments of those students afflicted by this
  material body, barren as a desert, with your
  spirituality which is learned in skilful means, guiding
  them on the excellent path where the doctrine and
  materialism are not mistaken.

Henceforth, may we once more be granted the good
  fortune of your swift rebirth as a gracious supreme
  guru and unsurpassed emanation,
As a glorious offering on behalf of those who uphold
  the immaculate excellent tradition, which is the aural
  lineage and the teaching of Lord Manjushri.

May you swiftly come as a peerless lion of speech
To maintain, protect, and expand with learning,
  nobility, and excellence, the three aspects of study,
  reflection, and meditation, and the three aspects of
  teaching, debate, and composition,
Associated with the infinite ocean of textual traditions
  belonging to the sutra and mantra (vehicles).

May the blessings of the spirituality of the three precious jewels, the profound powers of the enlightened activity possessed by mighty guardians, and our prayers, voiced in anguish, combined together, swiftly accomplish their desired purpose.

May all living creatures experience, without separation, the genuine guru and the glory of the doctrine, and having well perfected the enlightened attributes of the ground and the path, may they swiftly obtain the level of Vajradhara.

This prayer was composed by Lobsang Gyaltsen on the twentieth day of the third month of the Iron-Horse year (14 May 1990).

Bibliography

Bell, C., *Portrait of the Dalai Lama*, Collins, London, 1946

Dhardo Rimpoche, *Indo-Tibet Buddhist Cultural Institute School Report 1954–62*, ITBCI, Kalimpong, India, 1962

Dhardo Rimpoche, *Indo-Tibet Buddhist Cultural Institute School Report 1963*, ITBCI, Kalimpong, India, 1963

Govinda, Lama Anagarika, *The Way of the White Clouds*, Rider & Co., London, 1966

Hicks, R. & Chogyam, N., *Great Ocean*, Element Books, Shaftesbury, 1984

Huc, Abbe, *The Land of the Lamas*, Oxford University Press, London

Nebesky-Wojkowitz, R. von, *Where the Gods are Mountains*, Weidenfield & Nicolson, London, 1956

Sangharakshita, *The History of My Going For Refuge*, Windhorse, Glasgow, 1988

Sangharakshita, *The Thousand-Petalled Lotus*, Alan Sutton, London, 1988

Sangharakshita, *Ambedkar and Buddhism*, Windhorse, Glasgow, 1986

Taring, R.D., *Daughter of Tibet*, Murray, London, 1970

Wallace, B. Alan, *The Life and Teaching of Geshe Rabten*, Allen & Unwin, London, 1980

Glossary

Atisha: A great Indian Buddhist teacher of the tenth/ eleventh century. He taught in Tibet where he had a profound influence on the development of Buddhism.

bhikshu (Sanskrit), (Pali *bhikkhu*): Those who have left a home life, donned the traditional monastic robes, shaved their heads, and live a celibate life. Called *gelong* in Tibetan.

Bodhisattva (Sanskrit): 'Being of Enlightenment'. (1) A person who has cultivated some degree of compassion and wisdom, and vowed to attain Enlightenment for the sake of others. (2) Often used in the sense of a symbolic being who represents a particular quality of the Enlightened mind. Their representations may be human or non-human, peaceful or wrathful.

Dalai Lama: A Mongolian title meaning 'Great Ocean', and applied to the spiritual and temporal head of the Tibetan peoples. The title refers not to one person but more to the lineage of lamas who, through successive incarnations, take up that office. The Dalai Lama is seen as an embodiment of Avalokiteshvara, the Bodhisattva of Compassion.

Dharma (Sanskrit): Used here in two of its many senses: (1) The complete body of the Buddha's teaching, and (2) the path which leads to the perfect unfoldment of Wisdom and Compassion.

Dharmachari (*m*); Dharmacharini (*f*) (Sanskrit: Farer in the Truth): A member of the Western Buddhist Order. Its male and female members are ordained upon committing themselves wholeheartedly to a full-time practice of the Dharma. They do not generally wear robes or hold to the many detailed rules of the monastic sanghas.

gelong (Tibetan): see *bhikkhu*

gompa (Tibetan): Literally means 'Place of Meditation', and should be reserved to denote a hall for meditation and *puja*. However it is more commonly used to denote a complete monastic complex. In this sense it is roughly equivalent to the Sanskrit *vihara*, meaning a place of residence for *bhikkhus* or *bhikkhunis*.

initiation: *abhisheka* (Sanskrit) or 'bestowal' of power (hence also translated as empowerment). Refers to the ceremony during which a lama communicates the inspiration necessary for meditation upon a Buddha or Bodhisattva figure.

Insight: *vipashyana* (Sanskrit). Transcendental realization of the nature of Reality which comes about as a result of practice of the Buddhist path and, especially, meditation. This is not a mundane or intellectual understanding, but one which penetrates to the heart of things and permanently transforms our mistaken views.

Mahayana (Sanskrit): The 'Great Vehicle' of Buddhism, whose followers seceded from the so-called 'Hinayanists', or followers of the 'Lesser Vehicle', during the first five hundred years of Buddhist history. The Mahayanists emphasized the ideal of the Bodhisattva, who had limitless compassion.

mandala (Sanskrit): A ritual circle which usually outlines a mythic palace, or residence, of a particular Buddha or Bodhisattva. Mandalas are used extensively in initiation ceremonies to introduce the initiate to the resident of the mandala.

mantra (Sanskrit): The sacred sound symbols of a Buddha or Bodhisattva, access to whom is given through their recitation and contemplation.

oracle-priests: Tibetan Buddhism incorporated elements from the pre-existing culture, in which oracle-priests probably had their origin. It is said that a particularly powerful spirit is associated with each one, by whose grace he communicates his wisdom, prophesies, and warnings.

Pali: The name now given to a vernacular which existed in the Magadha region of India at the time when the 'Pali Texts' were committed to writing. These were preserved by the Theravada Buddhists of south-east Asia.

pandit cap: These pointed caps (not to be confused with the tall woollen caps similar to those of the Imperial Roman Army) were worn by Buddhist monks in medieval India while debating or teaching. Red and yellow ones are still use by Tibetan lamas.

puja: The act of worship or veneration. In Indian tradition one venerates one's father and mother, elders worthy of respect, and gods. In the Buddhist tradition *puja* is made towards the Buddha and Bodhisattvas, and is not associated with the worship of a god.

Refuges and Precepts: The Buddhist values three things above all else: the Buddha—the ideal of Enlightenment, the Dharma—the teaching and path to that ideal, and the Sangha—the community of those who are practising the teachings. These three are seen as offering a true refuge from the madness of the world. There are five fundamental precepts of ethical conduct which are observed by all Buddhists. These involve abstention from: harming living beings, taking the not-given, sexual misconduct, false speech, and the use of intoxicants.

Sanskrit: One of the languages of ancient India in one form of which Buddhist texts were written. Much of the Sanskrit Buddhist canon survives only in its Tibetan, Chinese, Japanese, Mongolian, and Korean translations.

stupa: A Buddhist reliquary monument whose various architectural sections are highly symbolic. These sections are associated with each of the elements (earth, water, fire, air, and space), the human body, and the Buddha. The *stupa* takes many forms, including the Chinese pagoda and the Tibetan *chorten*. A *stupa* may take the form of a tiny ornament on a shrine, or a structure hundreds of feet high, as with some of the Sinhalese *dagabas*.

sutra (Sanskrit), (Pali *sutta*): The name given to texts which are generally purported to contain the word of the Buddha.

Shunyata (Sanskrit): Applied to all 'things' and 'events' of the phenomenal world to indicate that they are 'empty' of self-nature. The realization of this truth enables one to see beyond the mere surface of things and to recognize the flux of conditions which gives rise to our mistaken view of solid and permanent entities. It shatters the assumption that because we name something, it exists as such. In reality no such 'thing' exists, only a flux of conditions.

Tantra (Sanskrit): The teachings of the form of Buddhism called *Mantrayana* (Vehicle of Sacred Sound) or *Vajrayana* (the Diamond Vehicle). The texts, or Tantras, contain teachings couched in highly symbolic language, to the extent that one requires a teacher well versed in their symbolic language to decipher then. They deal for the most part with the elaborate visualization rituals of the Vajrayana.

Tushitaloka: One of the heaven-realms. Traditional Buddhist cosmology sees a multiplicity of worlds and 'realms' existing throughout infinite space, and in subtler dimensions than our fleshly eyes can perceive. Though a Buddha or Bodhisattva may be said to teach in some of them, the Buddhist's goal is not some ethereal heaven, but the attainment of Enlightenment, a state in which one has woken up to the impermanence of all worlds, and to the ultimate unsatisfactoriness of anything short of Transcendental attainment.

Theravada Buddhism: The form of Buddhism which exists primarily in south-east Asia. The Buddhists of this school hold to a strand of teaching which developed early in Buddhist history. Theravada Buddhism was also one of the many schools of what was perjoratively called the Hinayana or 'Small Vehicle' by followers of the Mahayana. The Mahayanists held that followers of the Hinayana schools were aiming at a lesser, more individualist goal. In all probability, if one examined their teachings, one would find there were no actual Hinayana 'schools', but only practitioners who were limited in their vision of the implications of their own school's teachings.

unskilful action: Action in Buddhism is never seen as being absolutely good or bad. Rather, the more helpful concept of skill and unskill is applied, implying that our actions should not only express love and kindness, but also awareness, mindfulness, and care.

Untouchable: In Hindu society all people are born into one of the four great *varnas* or 'caste groupings'. At the top are the Brahmins, who are traditionally the religious caste; below come the Khastriyas, the warrior and ruling caste; then come the Vaishyas, or the merchant caste; at the bottom are the Shudras, the menial caste. Beneath these classes of people come those who are regarded as being outside caste altogether. They are considered to be so impure that they can pollute others with no more than a touch. Untouchables are actually regarded as sub-human. The Buddha strongly condemned such an inhumane system. Although Untouchability has now been outlawed by the Indian Constitution for several decades, its practice is still common especially in rural India. Today, of the 117,000,000 'ex-Untouchables', it is believed that upwards of 10,000,000 have converted to Buddhism.

vajra (Sanskrit): Literally 'diamond' and also 'thunderbolt'. In Tantric Buddhism the *vajra* is a symbol for the penetrating wisdom which cuts to the heart of things, and for Reality itself, and is sometimes used during rituals as a kind of sceptre.

Vajrayana (Sanskrit): The 'Diamond Vehicle' of Buddhism. The last great phase in the development of Buddhism in India from the fifth to the eleventh centuries. The Vajrayana's great concern was to bring the practice of Buddhism out of the speculative realms in which it had dwelt for so many centuries, and turn it back into something immediate and tangible. It incorporated rituals culled from various sources, as means of realizing the great potential within every human being.